FOOTBALL'S

MULTIPLE-MOTION I OFFENSE

FOOTBALL'S

MULTIPLE-MOTION I OFFENSE

Jack Beverlin

Parker Publishing Company, Inc.
West Nyack, New York

© 1982 by

Parker Publishing Company, Inc.

West Nyack, New York

Library of Congress Cataloging in Publication Data
Beverlin, Jack
　　Football's multiple-motion I offense.

　　1. Football—Offense.　2. Football coaching.
I. Title.
GV951.8.B48　　　796.332'2　　　81-18746
ISBN 0-13-324145-9　　AACR2

Printed in the United States of America

Dedication

To my most loyal fan, my wife of 13 years, Judy.

Offensive Excitement with the Multiple-Motion I Offense

The *Multiple-Motion I Offense* provides you the coach with an offensive package that produces high scoring results. Offensive cohesiveness and efficiency are ingrained throughout the designs of the offensive sets and formations. Because of the multiple sets and the use of motion, this offense takes tremendous advantage of the defense. In detail, the Multiple-Motion I Offense describes the sequential calling of plays to exploit defensive weaknesses. Tactically, this book presents a sequential series of plays on how to attack a defense with the use of motion by calling highly effective offensive plays for the appropriate game-like situation.

The *Multiple-Motion I Offense* uses motion to establish a multitude of formations and sets. Moreover, by using motion, a few consistent plays can be run from different sets (alignments) to produce a multiple-problem offense for the defense. The offense, however, is able to produce a high level of offensive execution since it has a limited amount of simple plays to learn and practice. In addition, passing can be refined because your quarterback will know how to attack the secondary prior to snapping the ball. Is the strong safety covering motion with man or is the secondary rotating back to the motion?

Motion makes the defense more predictable. Are they playing zone? Man? Motion enables the QB to read secondaries easier and establish a sound, simple, audible system. Goal-line offenses have the luxury of seeing goal-line defenses' adjustments without snapping the ball. Because of the use of motion, defenses must adjust prior to the snap of the ball, allowing the offense to recognize defensive alignments.

The *Multiple-Motion I Offense* uses the I-formation as its backbone of structure. The "I" provides versatility for line-blocking and reading of the blocking schemes by the backs. For that purpose alone, the I-formation serves as the *base* of the *Multiple-Motion I Offense*. In addition to the base offense (I-formation), the *Multiple-Motion I Offense* incorporates the veer; sprint draw series; wing-T series; passing series of sprint-out, roll-out, and drop-back; isolation series; slot-I; double wing; option series, etc., in a highly organized and easy-to-understand design whose efficiency eliminates confusion. Because of these various offensive concepts, defensive preparation becomes more difficult. Less stunts and defensive adjustments are planned because the *Multiple-Motion I Offense* presents such a diversified attack. The defenses are simply presented with too many offensive threats. The defenses are forced to sit back rather than attack due to the defense-control qualities of the *Multiple-Motion I Offense*.

Balance destroys a defense. This sentence is echoed by many top collegiate coaches. You can gear a defense for an opponent mentally and physically much better when there is one basic offensive look to prepare for. For example, a good defense will try to force you out of your wishbone by playing multiple 8-9 man fronts. Defenses can prepare more stunts, more blitzes, more defensive looks, thus creating confusion and lack of confidence among your offensive performers. Motion with the use of multiple formations enables the offense to take the momentum away from the defense. The defense loses its flexibility on stunts and slants. Conversely, the offense makes the defense bear the pressure and shoulder more keys, responsibilities, tendencies, etc. Thus, the defense has to become more predictable, enabling the *Multiple-Motion I Offense* to control defenses and exploit their weaknesses.

The *Multiple-Motion I Offense* forces the defense into a bind. In order to play "sound" defense, the defense has to be simple, simply to adjust, or big plays will evolve. Moreover, opposing scouts and coaches will be perplexed as they attempt to chart your tendencies, which can mount to hundreds of variations.

Many say football must be kept simple. I reply that if you are blessed with talent, you can afford to be anything you want until you meet an equally talented team. I say be multiple with a system of presenting different sets or formations, all sequenced in unison, and run your bread-and-butter plays at alarmed, confused defenses. The *Multiple-Motion I Offense*, however, is not the selection of plays at random, but is specifically designed offense whose well coordinated play series and well planned philosophy complement one another to control defenses and produce an effective, high scoring offensive attack.

Jack Beverlin

Contents

1

Installing Football's Multiple-Motion I Offense

Football changes in cycle form—single-wing, split-T, wishbone, veer. Offenses are always trying to stay one up on defenses by going into new phases as the defenses catch up to the old. Offenses have changed just as equipment, stadiums and national exposure on football have changed. But as each new offense appears, one point must be agreed upon—change occurred because the defense has found the offense predictable.

Unpredictability is the key concept in the *Multiple-Motion I Offense*. The defense must be off-balance so that the offensive unit can score. The I-formation is the base formation for developing an unpredictable offense. The I-formation provides versatility for the offensive linemen. Offensive blocking is the most difficult aspect of playing football. The I-formation provides the offensive lineman a luxury no other offense can offer—the flexibility of blocking his man in any direction.

Moreover, the I-formation gives the QB the ability to roll-out, sprint-out, or drop-back in passing the football. Because of this very feature of the I-formation, multiplicity occurs. The I-formation with various sets and the use of motion can appear as several offenses in which to make the defense *predictable*.

Balance is a word that is heard not only in football circles, but is referred to as the winning ingredient in any team sport. Can you pass as well as you can run? Can you run inside as well as you can outside? Is your trap play as successful as your off-tackle play? Can defenses plan a game plan around your offensive attack—veer, wishbone, pro set, etc.? We want balance and the Multiple-Motion I Offense provides that balance—the ability to attack a defense with offensive weapons that are unpredictable to defense.

Defenses are becoming more and more sophisticated. The offense faces tremendous disadvantages in attacking a defense. The most glaring disadvantage is the offensive lineman trying to block a myriad of stunts, slants, blitzes, without the use of his hands. However, the usage of many sets or formations through the use of motion makes defenses uncomfortable and reduces them to their basic defensive scheme—which is predictable. Recognition is a key concept in preparing a defense to stop a particular offensive attack. Recognition becomes almost impossible with the *Multiple-Motion I Offense.* The offense attacks rather than being attacked.

Why motion? Motion enables us to become double-wing, unbalanced, power I, wing-T, and so forth without learning a multitude of terms and diagrams. Motion is unpredictable in itself. When a man goes in motion, he can do so many things that the defense has to remain somewhat basic. Will the man-in-motion shift to a wing-T look? slot back? power back? twin receiver? option back?

Football is a game of fun. If you're losing, fun becomes almost extinct when that veer attack, for example, is faced with a passing situation. But if you're losing and employing a multiple-motion I attack, your chances of winning always seem somewhat more realistic and therefore hopeful, which makes football fun. Why hopeful? The offense is dictating to the defense not vice versa. Offense means to attack with aggressiveness. The *Multiple-Motion I Offense* gives you that aggressor role.

TERMINOLOGY

Understanding terminology is vital for the success of any program. The following are terms that must be understood in implementing the *Multiple-Motion I Offense.*

CLOSE: Flanker (Z) aligns 1 yard outside tight end (Y).

FLEX: Tight end (Y) moves outside to a wide receiver position.

TIGHT: Split end (X) moves into a tight end position.

COUNTER: This is a mis-direction play.

COUNTER OPTION: QB either running or pitching ball to back after counter fake.

DIVE: A straight hand-off to first back.

DIVE OPTION: QB either running or pitching ball to back after dive fake.

DRAW: Slow developing run off a pass fake.

LEAD: Near back blocking through hole called.

OPTION: QB either running or pitching ball to back.

OUTSIDE VEER: A play where defensive end determines whether dive back gets ball or if QB keeps and options.

REVERSE: A slow developing mis-direction play away from flow.

TOSS: Pitch to back sweeping around end.

TRAP: Guard or tackle pulling across center's hips and blocking out on free defensive lineman.

VEER: A play where first man outside offensive tackle determines whether dive back gets ball or if QB keeps and options.

GAP: A blocking call to determine wedge blocking.

BASE: 0—1—2—3 blocking

"IF" RULE: Guard—Block 1 if over or outside; otherwise 2. Tackle—Block 2 if over or outside; otherwise 3.

GAP STACK RULE: Double team at point of attack.

LEAD: Cross block at hole. Down man blocked first.

REACH: Block man head-up or in outside gap with hook technique.

TED: Special blocking on veer where tight end (Y) blocks down on first LBer inside.

CHEAT: Moving to a position other than normal for the purpose of gaining a better blocking or running angle.

CLUTCH: An audible by QB whereby the QB passes the ball out-of-bounds to stop the clock.

COVER: After a pass, line moves laterally so as to be able to tackle any possible interceptor of the pass.

EVEN: A defensive spacing with no one over or head-up on center.

ODD: A defensive spacing with someone on or over center.

FLANKER: A back set outside of end's normal position.

FORCE: The defensive back responsible for filling the flat area against the run.

GREEN: Always denotes pass-off of a run fake (play action pass).

HOT: If LBer fires, tight end (Y) looks for pass immediately.

ON-SIDE: On-side refers to the side of the line that the play is being run to. The on-side is often referred to as the play-side.

OFF-SIDE: Off-side refers to the side of the line that the play is *not* being run to.

PLAY ACTION PASS: Pass thrown with deception at hole called.

POCKET PASS: QB drops directly back of center to pass.

SPRINT-OUT PASS: QB sprints left or right to pass.

PEEL: A block whereby a blocker goes to a point beyond an opponent, then circles back making contact *above waist* and cutting off pursuit.

RELEASE: Lineman sprinting for a downfield block getting over in front of ball carrier.

SERIES: Plays wherein backfield movements are essentially the same.

STACK: Linebacker lining up behind a defensive lineman.

TECHNIQUE: Proper method and skill in carrying out assignments.

POA: Point of attack for an offensive play.

LOS: Line of scrimmage.

BACKFIELD ALIGNMENTS

There are four backfield alignments used in the *Multiple-Motion I Offense*. These four are base, split, far, and near. (See Diagram 1-1.)

The base backfield alignment in Diagram 1-1 is the *only* backfield alignment that is never called in a specific play. The players know that if a

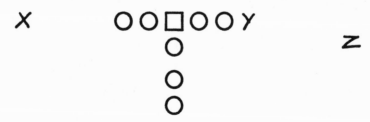

Diagram 1-1: Base Backfield

play is called without a split, far, or near, they will line up in the base backfield alignment. The base alignment calls for the fullback to be three yards deep (all depth is determined from ball to hands of backs) and the RB (running back or tailback) five and one-half yards deep.

The split backfield alignment in Diagram 1-2 is where the two backs split to a position where each are four yards deep and are vertically aligned to the outside hip of the offensive guards. The FB always goes to direction called and RB always goes away. (Direction will be explained later in the formations.)

The far backfield alignment in Diagram 1-3 is the FB remaining in his base position (three yards depth) but the RB lining up in a split position (four yards depth and outside hip of offensive guard). RB always lines up away from direction called.

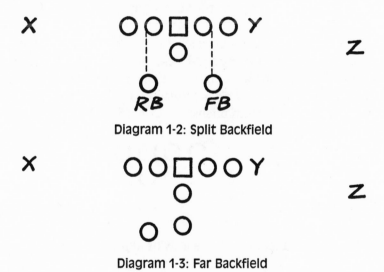

Diagram 1-2: Split Backfield

Diagram 1-3: Far Backfield

The near backfield alignment in Diagram 1-4 is exactly the same as the far alignment except for one change. RB lines up in his split position to the direction called.

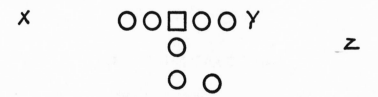

Diagram 1-4: Near Backfield

FORMATIONS

All formations in the *Multiple-Motion I Offense* are based on direction—right or left. Right, for example, tells tight-end (Y) and flanker (Z) to line up in their respective positions to the right side. Split-end (X) always lines up in his position away from direction called. See Diagram 1-5.

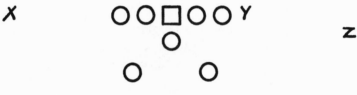

Diagram 1-5: Split-Right

There are two formations in which Z does not go to direction called. These two fromations are twins and black. Whenever twins is called, Z aligns opposite direction called and positions himself five yards width from X. (See Diagram 1-6.) If black formation is called, Z aligns one yard deep and one yard wide from offensive tackle. (See Diagram 1-7.)

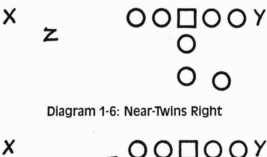

Diagram 1-6: Near-Twins Right

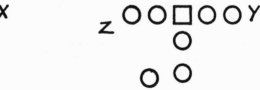

Diagram 1-7: Far-Black Right

PLAY-CALLING AND NUMBER SYSTEM

Plays are designated by a number or a number and name. If only a number, base blocking applies in the line. If number and name, the first number indicates series; second number indicates hole; and name indicates backfield maneuver and line blocking. All even-numbered plays are to the right of the center and all odd-numbered plays are to the left of the center. The offensive hole numbering is shown in Diagram 1-8.

9   ⑦ ⑤ ③ ⑩ ② ④ ⑥   8

Diagram 1-8: Hole Numbering

Lead, veer, counter, trap, and toss at the end of number always indicates the blocking scheme. Near, far, and split at the beginning of the number always refer to backfield alignments. Refer to Diagrams 1-2, 1-3, and 1-4. The following numbers refer to the offensive attack: teen series (14-15, 18-19)—sprint series attack; twenty series (22-23, 26-27, 28-29)— basic isolation, sweep plays, and option; thirty series (30-31, 34-35, 38-39)—trap, FB dive, and veer attack; forty series (40-41)—mis-direction plays; green before any number means play-action pass; and 60, 70, 80 are pass plays

Examples of play-calling in the *Multiple-Motion I Offense* are Diagrams 1-9 through 1-14.

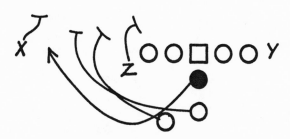

Diagram 1-9: Far-Black Right 19

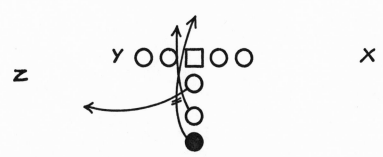

Diagram 1-10: Left 23 Lead

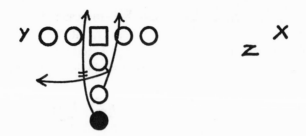

Diagram 1-11: Twins-Left 41 Counter

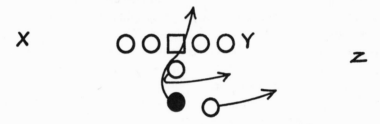

Diagram 1-12: Near-Right 30 Trap

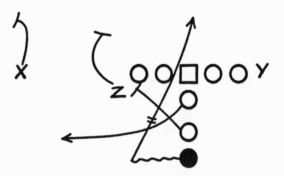

Diagram 1-13: Black-Right 15

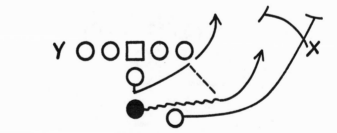

Diagram 1-14: Far-Left 28 Option

RULES FOR MOTION

In the *Multiple-Motion I Offense*, motion usually refers only to the flanker (Z). With the flanker in motion, you can change offensive sets dramatically without losing consistency. Moreover, the attack becomes diversified without spending hours on memorization.

Motion can be added to the *Multiple-Motion I Attack* simply by a third digit. If, for example, we are running a typical isolation play such as 22 Lead, we can add a third digit, 122 Lead, and run the same play, but the flanker will be in motion. The third digit will be either one or two. The 100 digit tells the flanker (Z) to go in motion to his *left*. The 200 digit tells the flanker (Z) to go in motion to his *right*. If the offense wants someone other than Z to go in motion, 300 and 400 digits are assigned to the FB along with 500 and 600 digits for the RB. If the digit is odd, the backs will go left. If the digit is even, the backs will go right. For example, if Left 633 was called, the RB would be motion to his right. (See Diagram 1-15.)

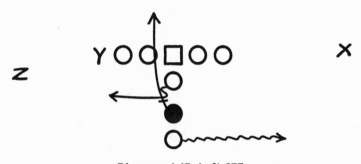

Diagram 1-15: Left 633

The tight-end (Y) can be in motion with the 700 or 800 digit. (Y), however, creates an adjustment that must be executed, or the offense will not have a legal 7-men on the LOS. This adjustment is for (Z) to align on the LOS (whenever he hears the 700 or 800 digit) and (Y) to align as a tight flanker near the tackle to the direction called in the play. (Y) goes in motion only when the 700 or 800 digits are used.

The QB initiates the motion with his heel. After setting up the offensive attack, the QB will raise the heel closest to the side of the motion-man and initiate the motion. Timing and direction of the motion are determined by the QB's command of the cadence.

The strategical advantages of motion are unlimited. Besides giving the coaching staff strategy sessions which are creative and challenging, the use of motion and the multiplicity it creates breeds and reinforces concentration among your players. The football team gets involved more in the X's and O's which helps your total team's concentration.

HUDDLE

The huddle formation is to facilitate the key concept in the offensive attack—make the defense predictable. We line up in the following formation so that we can *run* up to the LOS and go. (See Diagram 1-16). Important details of the huddle formation are:

1. Center forms huddle quickly with hands raised and approximately seven yards back of LOS.
2. Don't crowd or squeeze each other in the huddle.
3. Be calm, collected and relaxed while in huddle.
4. Absolute silence after the QB goes into the huddle.
5. Look at the QB's face and *concentrate* on what he says.
6. We insist that the huddle be compact and neat.
7. Stand on your feet; never lean on anyone.

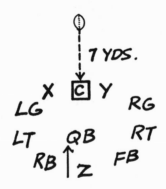

Diagram 1-16: Huddle Formation

The center, split end (X), and/or flanker (Z), if split out, will break huddle immediately after the snap count is given. Split end and the flanker will run from huddle to flanking position. There is never any need or excuse not to be ready. The QB hesitates after the snap count and then breaks the huddle with "Ready break." All remaining players clap hands and yell "Break" on QB's break. The players turn in and sprint to position on ball in a three point stance. Many defenses are taken back when an offense roars up the the LOS and is ready to go. Recognition of offensive set is difficult, and the addition of motion forces the defense to play basic.

SNAP COUNT

The snap count is simple. The cadence is Set, Hut 1, Hut 2, Hut 3. If nothing is said in the huddle, the count is always on one. The team fires out on Hut, not the one. For any other counts, set, 2, 3, they must be given in huddle. The cadence is always given in a non-rythmic voice. This means that there will be pauses between counts.

AUDIBLE SYSTEM

To audibilize, we use any color which is "live." Live means that only one color will designate a change of plans. Other colors given will be false cues. After the QB gives the color, a play will be given, then the snap count. If the snap count in the huddle is on Set, we never audibilize for the team will go on the first sound. The QB's are given only a few plays to audibilize. With the multiple attack and promptness in lining up on the LOS, there will be very few defenses that we need to audibilize with.

Examples of audible-type plays would be as follows:

Live Color—Orange.
Play Call—Right 30 Trap.
Count—On 2.

Orange—Near Right 84 Flood, pause, Set, Hut 1, Hut 2, Hut 3.

The play was changed to Near-Right 84 Flood for any one of several reasons depending on scouting reports and pre-game QB meetings. But the color used was Orange and that meant an audible or a play change.

Live Color—Orange.
Play Call—Left 23 Lead.
Count—Hut 1.

Blue—Left 83 Flood, pause, Set, Hut 1.

We would still run Left 23 Lead since blue was given as the color at the LOS. Orange was the live color. The QBs will do the audibile system infrequently throughout the game. The *Multiple-Motion I Offense* is an offense that requires very few adjustments at the LOS because of the multiple problems that confront the defense.

2

Line Blocking for the Run

Regardless of any offensive attack, offensive line play is your key to success. The idea of offensive blocking is to gain *width*, not depth. We plan the *Multiple Motion I* running plays with width as our objective at the point of attack.

Stressing width at the point of attack should not be interpreted as encouraging the linemen not "to fire off the LOS." Certainly, we want unified explosiveness in the line as they approach the neutral zone. But we do not want the linemen to attempt to drive their man five yards deep. This is not a realistic goal. Blocking a man five yards deep only occurs with practice dummies. Moreover, the POA is deep and narrow. I-formation needs width to give the offensive backs any creativity.

The offensive linemen are taught simple and basic blocking techniques through a drill teaching progression that is based on a maximum amount of repetitions. The linemen are given very few blocking techniques, but many defensive looks to recognize. The basic block is the drive block with the *rip* technique. Attack your man shoulder high on opponents' numbers. Slide head to nearest side of POA. After sliding head, rip outside arm for shoulder turn seal. Seal is a term used quite often in blocking schemes. Seal for line play means to get your hips turned so that your defensive man is standing horizontally away from onside action. The linemen are encouraged to attack above the waist for most running plays. If a lineman blocks any lower, his head goes down and if the head is down, the body ends up on the ground. How many times have you seen linemen explode into their blocks and fall on their knees? For this very reason we *never* use the explosion or extension drill that is so popular among high school and college coaches.

STANCE

We want all of the linemen in a 3-pt. stance. The *Multiple-Motion I Offense* requires maneuverability for the offensive lineman. The 3-pt.

stance allows this maneuverability more readily than the 4-pt. stance. The 3-pt. stance is much the same that most football levels utilize. The feet are together in a toe to heal relationship. If the person is right-handed, the right foot is back. If he is left-handed, the left foot is back. The feet are widened to shoulder width with the same toe to heal relationship. The placement of the feet is very important in a good offensive stance. If the feet are wider than the shoulders, the player will be slow off the ball. If the feet are too close together, the player will lose his balance. The player must squat into a baseball catcher's position. The body weight is equally distributed on the balls of the feet. In the catcher's position, cross the arms. The fingers of the right hand are on the left shoulder; the fingers of the left hand are on the right shoulder. Place the elbows between the knees and adjust the legs so that they are straight. If the elbows push the knees out, move legs out until feet and knees are in the same vertical plane or perpendicular to the ground. If the elbows do not push the knees, adjust the knees to the elbows, keeping the feet and knees perpendicular to the ground. The feet should be parallel or toed-in; the heels are never in. A player will get all his leg drive from the balls of his feet, not his heels. The player should drop the hand that corresponds with the back foot. There is very little weight on the hand. The hand, knee, and foot are all in a straight line, always having the knees directly over the feet. The down hand is extended about six inches in front of the foot, still keeping the hand, knee, and foot in a straight line. As the hand is extended, the buttocks will rise so that it is slightly higher than the shoulders. This raises the weight and the heel cleats will be off the ground. The head is up so that the lineman can see the numbers on a defensive halfback's jersey. The neck is bulled. A lineman will make contact with his shoulder.

The linemen are expected to have their free arm along-side the leg, not on the top of the knee. There are two reasons for this, First it prevents the player from resting on his leg as he gets tired in the latter stages of the game. Secondly, when a lineman "comes" out of his stance, his arm is at the side of his body, so why not start there.

SPACING

Many coaches describe their line spacing or splits to the exact foot or inch. "Our guard and center split is two feet, guard and tackle is three feet, etc." Our feeling is that the linemen cannot measure two feet or three feet as they approach the LOS, regardless of the training devices you use. We simply tell the linemen to be split so that a man can stand between you and your teammate (interior linemen only). The only exceptions to the spacing rule are the gap block and the kicking game. On gap blocking we tell the linemen foot-to-foot. Field goals, points after touchdowns, and punts are standard kicking rules.

NUMBERING DEFENSES—BASES

We coach the linemen to recognize defenses. Our philosophy is that effective offensive linemen are people who can recognize the defense and know the way to block it. We give the linemen thorough lessons in numbering defenses because we want them to have something to fall back on if failure in recognizing the defense occurs.

Base blocking is the system used for numbering defenses. Base always refers to blocking your man. Center blocks O man. Guards block 1 man. Tight end (Y) blocks 3 man. Linebackers are counted along with the down-linemen in determining blocking assignemtns. A typical base blocking scheme is displayed in Diagram 2-1.

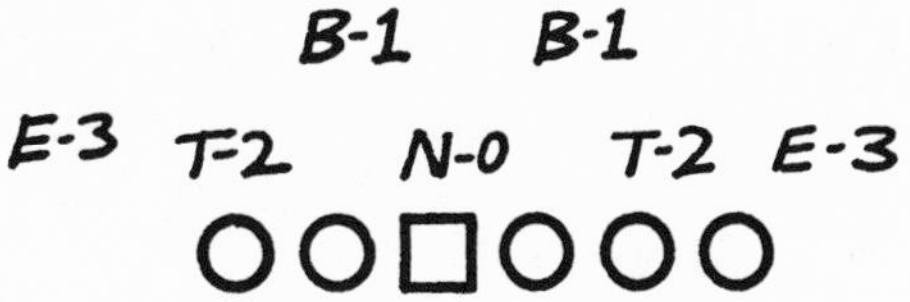

B-1   **B-1**

E-3 **T-2**   **N-0**   **T-2** **E-3**

O O □ O O

Diagram 2-1: Base Blocking

"IF"

There are defenses, however, which represent difficulty in blocking just base. Therefore, we add "If" to the base blocking scheme. "If" means center block O or offside; guard blocks 1 if over or outside; otherwise 2. Tackle blocks 2 if over or outside; otherwise 3. The "If" rule applies to the backside linemen only. An example of the "If" rule is shown in Diagram 2-2 against the 4–4 Defense.

Diagram 2-2 specifically illustrates the need for an "If" rule. The reason being that if base blocking were used on the 4-4 Defense, the off-side guard would block No. 1 man and the off-side tackle would block the No. 2 man, leaving the defensive end (No. 3 man) unblocked. By applying the "If" rule, all offensive men are assigned defenders.

The "If" rule is an easy cue for the linemen to implement. But this

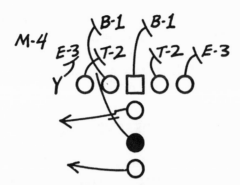

Diagram 2-2: If Blocking vs. 4-4

rule only serves to remind the linemen all the more that *recognition of defense* is still the most important ingredient in successful blocking. The "If" rule can be broken just as any blocking rule can be broken. Many coaches have blocking rules such as— "Gap-Head Up-Offside" —for their plays. Within a short time of coaching your linemen a system such as this, you run into defenses which can be labeled as—"Gap-Head Up-Offside"—but your point of attack is nil. So you tell the player that the rules don't quite apply here, we'll have to block this 5-2 eagle stack this way, etc. Why not begin in the first part of the season teaching your lineman how to recognize defenses and continue throughout the season? Because if you don't, your half-time chalk talks on line adjustments will be falling on inexperienced ears.

An old Chinese proverb exemplifies our offensive line philosophy in the *Multiple-Motion I Offense:*

You hear; you forget.
You see; you remember.
You do; you know.

Our blocking schemes are broken into these categories: lead, counter, toss, trap, sprint, veer, and wedge.

LEAD BLOCKING

The first series in the *Multiple-Motion I Offense* that we teach the linemen is the lead or isolation series. The lead series is to the I offense as the fullback give is to the wishbone. It is a basic running play that is not run enough among most I oriented teams. The University of Southern California demonstrates the effectiveness of the lead series more than any other football team in their nationally-ranked offense.

Out basic lead plays are 22-23 Lead (the mechanics of the backfield are detailed in Chapter 5). We block the lead two different ways. Both blocking schemes are based on how the center handles the nose guard on an odd defensive alignment. When blocking an even alignment, our blocking scheme remains the same.

The rules for blocking the lead series are:

On Tackle:	Block Gd's area except vs. 62, block 2.
On Guard:	Block T's area except vs. 62, block 1.
Center:	O; Off-side.
Off Guard:	1 over or outside; otherwise 2 ("If").
Off Tackle:	2 over or outside; otherwise 3 ("If").

If the nose guard cannot be blocked by the center alone, we adjust with the onside guard and center doubleteaming nose and on-side tackle blocking the defensive tackle. (See Diagram 2-3.)

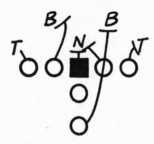

Diagram 2-3: Lead Blocking

The fullback has to block the LB'er without help. In the 4-4 scheme, we run into teams that adjust their defensive personnel as shown in Diagram 2-4. This defensive alignment has become quite popular in stopping option attacks.

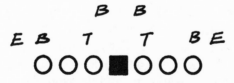

Diagram 2-4: 4-4 Defense

However, we attack this defense with lead plays that completely befuddle these defenses. We simply tell the tight end (Y) to release outside of the LB'er and screen block the defensive end. The on-side tackle caves down the defensive tackle, on-side guard pulls and kicks out LB'er who takes outside step when (Y) releases. (See Diagram 2-5.)

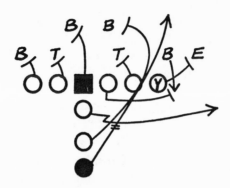

Diagram 2-5: Lead-Blocking 4-4

The fullback has plenty of room to block the LB'er and, more importantly, the tailback can run through a *wide* POA. The first time we faced this defense, the tailback set a school record with an 89 yard touchdown run on a 22 Lead. The lead series can be adjusted for changing points of attack because of the depth of the tailback in the I-formation and the usage of motion. (Chapter 5 describes why in more detail.)

We want width at the POA. In blocking for the 22-23 Lead, coach the linemen to cross-block when possible. Cross-blocking gives the linemen an angle for blocking that is conducive to our blocking philosophy.

Cross-blocking is taught with these rules in mind:

1. The offensive lineman who has the LBer over him always goes first. (Unless linebacker in on LOS.)
2. The offensive lineman who goes second must fold inside or outside of his teammate's block on the down lineman.
3. If there is an adjustment by the defense which leaves the two down defensive linemen over our onside linemen, the cross-block is automatically cancelled. The reason for the cancellation is that if the cross-block is used on two down-linemen, one of the down-linemen may be slanting in, and therefore the offensive blockers would be hard pressed to prevent a penetrating defender in the offensive backfield.

As mentioned in the blocking rules for the 22-23 Lead, we teach base blocking. But if the linemen *recognize* the defense as they approach the LOS, base blocking becomes cross-blocking at the POA. Because of the defensive difficulty in adjusting to the *Multiple-Motion I Offense*, cross-blocking in the 22-23 Lead becomes habit.

Diagrams 2-6 through 2-9 illustrate the blocking schemes for the 22-23 Lead against various defenses.

Diagram 2-6 is demonstrating a cross-block on a standard 5-2 Defense. This scheme is used only if the offensive center can handle the nose guard. If the center can't, the inside guard and center must double-team the nose guard. The onside tackle would block the defensive tackle (No. 2 man). The FB would block the LBer.

Diagram 2-7 illustrates the cross-block against a 5-2 Eagle Defense. The cross-block by the onside guard could be considered a fold block in this example. The onside tackle must block his man to prevent any backfield penetration.

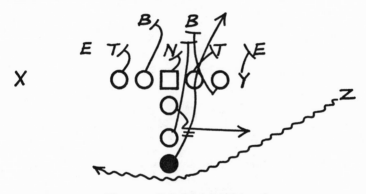

Diagram 2-6: Right 122 Lead

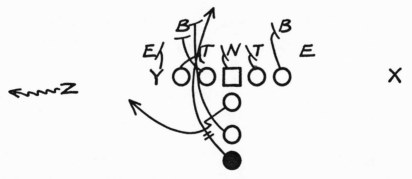

Diagram 2-7: Left 123 Lead

Diagram 2-8 illustrates the lead against a 6-2 Defense. There is no cross-block because of the 2 down-lineman at the POA.

Diagram 2-9 illustrates the cross-block against a 4-4 Defense. This defense, however, as previously discussed, doesn't include the normal cross-block. The onside guard pulls and blocks the defensive end. The onside tackle blocks down on the defensive tackle. The onside LBer is blocked by the FB.

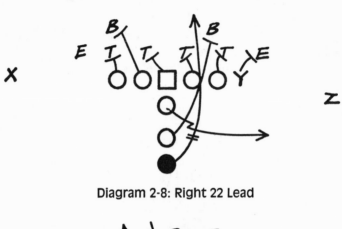

Diagram 2-8: Right 22 Lead

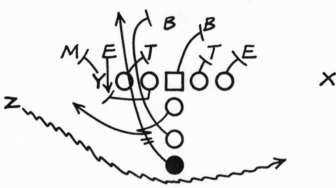

Diagram 2-9: Left 223 Lead

COUNTER BLOCKING

The *Multiple-Motion I Offense* employs the 40-41 counter as its inside misdirection play. On the 22-23 Lead versus 4-4 defense, we block the defensive end with the onside guard pulling. (See Diagram 2-10.)

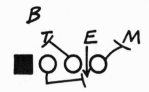

Diagram 2-10: Lead vs. 4-4

Blocking rules for the 40-41 counter are identical to the 22-23 Lead rules except when facing a 4-4 defense.

ONSIDE TACKLE: Fold block 1 if LBer; otherwise, block 2.
ONSIDE GUARD: Block 1 if 1 is down; otherwise, block 2.
CENTER: O; off-side.
OFFSIDE GUARD: "If."
OFFSIDE TACKLE: "If."

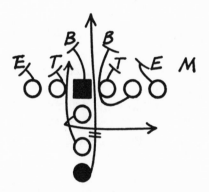

Diagram 2-11: Right 40 Counter

With the 40-41 Counter versus the 4-4 Defense, the onside guard and tackle block differently. The onside guard blocks the 2 man and the onside tackle folds inside to block LB'er (1 man). (See Diagram 2-11.)

Naturally, we are assuming that the LB'ers are taking one or more fake steps towards the direction of QB's and fullback's motion. When this occurs, onside tackle has an easy fold-block. Center's block, also, is an easy block when screening off the offside-Lb'er who has taken a step towards the fake.

This counter play is not a new play involving the I formation, but the blocking philosophy is. Undoubtedly, the 22-23 Lead plays' success determines the success of the counter and its blocking at the POA.

Because if the 22-23 Lead is not gaining yardage, the LB'ers will not be as anxious to flow towards initial movement of the ball when reacting to the 40-41 Counter. This movement is critical to insure our blocking schemes to have good blocking angles. Diagrams 2-12 through 2-17 demonstrate the blocking schemes versus 5-2 Eagle, 6-2, 4-3, and 5-3 Defense.

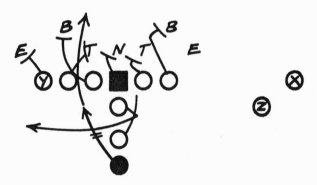

Diagram 2-12: Twins-Left 41 Counter

When confronting a 5-2 eagle defense, we must run the counters towards the side of the tight-end (Y). The reason being that the tight-end (Y) is the only one who can block the defensive-end. If we run a counter towards the split-end (X), the defensive-end is free to close down on our tailback as he enters the POA between guard-tackle's block. (See Diagram 2-13.)

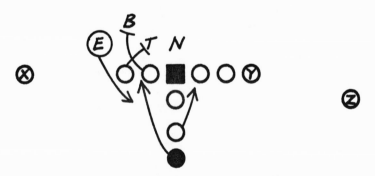

Diagram 2-13: Counter Without Y Block

A coaching point to remember when using cross-blocking or fold blocks is that if a LB'er is on the LOS, treat him as a down-lineman and block base.

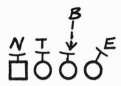

Diagram 2-14: Counter vs. Base

The 6-2 defense is the only time that the tight end (Y) folds inside the onside guard and tackle. Since the onside guard and tackle are confronted with a base blocking situation, the onside LB'er, who is the 2 man, must be fold-blocked by (Y) since the onside tackle cannot reach the LB'er. The defensive end does not get involved with the TB's running lane because of the onside tackle's block on the defensive tackle.

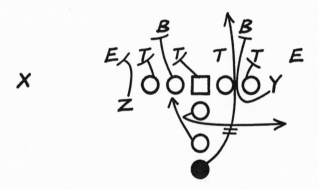

Diagram 2-15: Black-Left 40 Counter

The 4-3 Defense is very similar to the 6-2 Defense concerning the onside guard and tackle. They both block base with drive blocks. But the 4-3 has no LBer inside the guard-tackle, only the middle LBer over center. Therefore, the 41 Counter will go through the 1 hole (if 40 Counter, 0 hole) because of the natural running lane that is created by the false steps of the middle LBer when he reads flow the opposite way. The offensive center should be able to drive block and screen the middle LBer off from the running lane without any help. If we get a middle LBer who *keys* the center extremely well, we change-up with a center-guard blocking scheme. (See Diagram 2-16.) This movement with the center usually gets the middle LBer leaning the wrong direction, which enables the onside guard to seal off the LBer from the POA.

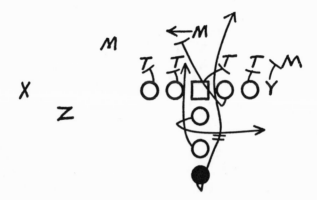

Diagram 2-16: Twins-Right 40 Counter

The 5-3 Defense is the defense that the offensive linemen enjoy most when a 40-41 Counter is called. The onside guard-tackle employ their cross and fold blocks as usual, except the LBer is not over the guard's area, but the center's. With the fake to the FB the opposite direction, the crucial block on the LBer by the onside tackle becomes less difficult because of the LBer's position and respect for the FB fake. Moreover, we attempt to confuse the middle LBer more by bringing down the offside guard on the nose. We not only are hoping for confusion on the LBer's part, but moreover, the nose guard will react to the double-team pressure and be too occupied with the fact that the tailback is running opposite of the double-team. (See Diagram 2-17.)

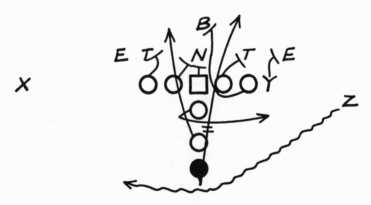

Diagram 2-17: Right 140 Counter

TOSS BLOCKING

The drive block with the rip technique is the basic block. However, another block that we utilize is the reach block on the toss series. The reach block is described by many coaches as the scramble block. We prefer reach because that is what you must do before scrambling on all fours.

The reach block is taught in the following steps: must step at a 45° angle with outside leg. The first step must not be too long or else the linemen will not have sufficient balance; as lineman comes off at a 45° angle, he must gather himself by bringing inside leg up under his body so that his body is under control; after stepping to get proper outside angle, the offensive lineman must prepare to hit opponent's outside hip with inside shoulder; once contact is made, the offensive lineman attempts to turn hips away from hole. This turning of the hips should place the offensive blocker's back to the POA, and if contact becomes more and more difficult to maintain, the lineman "scrambles" on all fours with the sole purpose of staying between his man and the ball carrier.

The rules for the 26-27 Toss Series are base. We ingrain in the linemen to reach block on their man, whereas their man would have to "run around" them from the inside in order for the lineman not to get a piece of that defense man. If base rules become confusing for the offensive linemen when blocking the toss, we explain that if no down-lineman is near you, always block onside LBer.

Diagrams 2-18 through 2-21 illustrate the toss series blocking.

Diagram 2-18 illustrates the toss play against a 4-4 Defense. The onside guard would not block the 1 man because of the defensive alignment. (As discussed earlier, *Multiple-Motion I Offense's* blocking

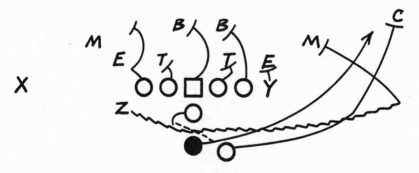

Diagram 2-18: Near-Black-Right 226 Toss

philosophy is *recognition of defenses*, not any set rules. Base blocking is used only as a back-up.) Therefore, he blocks the defensive tackle with a reach block. The onside tackle blocks the onside LBer with a drive block. Y would not need to reach block since the defensive end (No. 3 man) is inside of him. This defensive alignment by the No. 3 man would require a drive block by Y. The crackback block by Z on the monster would be fundamentally sound only if the monster would "walk-away" when confronted with a 2 receiver side because of Z's motion.

Diagram 2-19 illustrates the toss against a 5-2 Monster Defense. The onside linemen have easy recognition. The onside guard is blocking the LBer with a drive block. The onside guard's aiming point must be executed if he expects to cut off the quick flow of the onside LBer. The onside tackle and Y will reach block their defensive people. Y's reach block is a most difficult block against a well coached 5-2 defensive end. Y must remain on his feet and battle if the toss has any chance of succeeding.

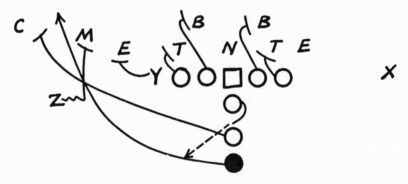

Diagram 2-19: Left 227 Toss

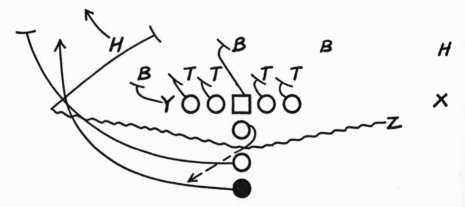

Diagram 2-20: Twins-Left 127 Toss

Diagram 2-20 illustrates the toss against a 6-1 Defense. All onside linemen have reach blocks except the center. The center just uses an excellent aiming point in order to cut off the quick, flowing LBer.

Diagram 2-21 illustrates the toss against a 6-2 Defense. The center doesn't have an onside LBer so he blocks the first man to show, that being the offside defensive tackle. The onside guard and tackle reach block on their people. The onside LBer will be blocked by Z if the defensive end doesn't "walk away" when Z goes in motion. If the defensive end "walks away" when Z is in motion, Z will crackback on the defensive end and the onside LBer will be blocked by the FB.

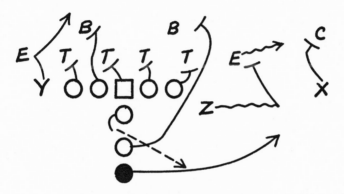

Diagram 2-21: Black-Left 226 Toss

As stated earlier, when running the 26 Toss against the 4-4 Defense, the onside tackle has an easy block on the LBer. (See Diagram 2-18.) Naturally, the onside tackle would not have to reach block in this situation, but drive block the LBer because of the inside blocking angle. Also, the onside tackle is not blocking base. If he did, his man would be the defensive tackle instead of the LBer and the onside guard would be blocking the LBer which would be nearly impossible. Even though the 26-27 Toss blocking rules are base, the main rule is *recognition of defense*. As soon as we see a 4-4 Defense, the linemen know that there is an exchange between onside guard and tackle. This blocking exchange also applies when confronted with any stacking or tandems.

TRAP BLOCKING

The trap block is a must for any sound offensive team. The trap play is the equalizer for defensive linemen who are roaring across the LOS without any concern for their deep penetration. The trap block, if run correctly, can make any lineman feel as an individual star. This psychological-lifting block is important for the anonymity that linemen play in. The fundamentals of the trap block are: take a quick, short step with inside foot and point toe directly toward spot to be trapped. Never raise the body up. Stay down and in a semi-coiled position. Drive off the forward foot, still taking short steps. The third step should be directed so that at the time of contact, the blocker can drive his foot, corresponding to the hitting shoulder, in the center of the defensive man's stance. As the offensive man approaches contact, he should direct his head downfield between his opponent and the LOS, driving his shoulder into the midsection of the defensive man. The foot opposite the hitting shoulder should be manuevered beyond the defensive man. This will prevent the defensive man from sliding off the block away from the LOS to tackle the ball carrier. The blocker should continue to keep contact by moving his feet to maintain his foot position.

The rules for the 30-31 Trap are as follows:

ONSIDE TACKLE:	Block first LB'er on side of play; vs. 6-2, block out.
ONSIDE GUARD:	Block O; offside; turn out.
CENTER:	Block down-lineman in offside guard's area; if none, block O.
OFFSIDE GUARD:	Pull, trap first down-lineman beyond center.
OFFSIDE TACKLE:	Block first man head-up to outside.

Diagrams 2-22 through 2-24 illustrate the 30-31 trap rules vs. several defenses.

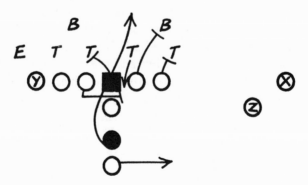

Diagram 2-22: Twins-Left 30 Trap

When calling the 30-31 Trap, we would rather see an even defense than an odd defense. The reason being that in an even defense, the down-

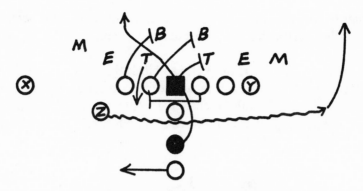

Diagram 2-23: Black-Right 231 Trap

lineman who is being trapped has a more difficult time recognizing the trap block. This defensive lineman has very little time to recognize the offside guard coming down or blocking out. Whereas, in the odd defense, the trap man, usually being the 5-2 defensive tackle, has more time to adjust to the trapping block since he is farther from the POA than an even defensive tackle.

In Diagram 2-24, the offside guard and center block differently than usual. The reason is that the nose guard is slanting in the direction of the center's path towards the offside LB'er. If the center would ignore the nose guard, he would not be blocked and our play would have very little chance of success. Therefore, the center rip blocks the nose guard

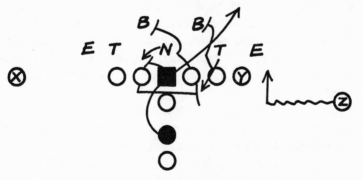

Diagram 2-24: Right 130 Trap

with very little difficulty since the nose guard's own motion is used against him. The offside guard, who is angling towards the nose guard, continues on the same path and blocks the offside LB'er because of the nose guard's "disappearance." this blocking scheme is accomplished with very little difficulty as long as the center and the offside guard *recognize* the *defense.*

As mentioned earlier, we prefer to block the 30-31 trap against an even defense. But, if we are continually seeing odd defenses and we know that they "sit in them" without changing fronts, we will adjust the trap blocking scheme so that we can block more effectively the difficult 5-2 defensive tackle. (See Diagram 2-25.)

Diagram 2-25: Influence Trap Block

Diagram 2-25 shows that instead of the onside tackle blocking the onside LB'er, he simply steps out and blocks the defensive end. The tight-end would then come down on the onside linebacker. If the defensive tackle reads the onside tackle's head and attempts to follow the influence of our tackle, the defensive tackle will create width (which is always our objective) and permit our trap man to get between him and the ball carrier. Of course, if the onside tackle gets tied up with the defensive tackle and cannot block the defensive end, there will be no concern because the defensive end should be screened out of the play by the defensive and offensive tackles' bodies. The trapping guard would then turn upfield and block the first man to appear. The tight-end has an easy block on the onside LB'er. However, if the LB'er should react quickly and fire, the trapping guard would treat him as the first down lineman past center and block appropriately.

When confronting an odd defense that shifts its defensive tackle into an eagle look (defensive tackle over offensive guard and LB'er over offensive tackle) against the split-end side, we always trap toward the tight-end side or call close in the huddle and align with a double tight-end arrangement. The reason for this preference in running the trap play is that if a defensive end is crashing in, there is no one to block him because of the absence of a tight-end. Therefore, to prevent a bone-jarring tackle in the backfield, the trap is always run to Y's side.

SPRINT BLOCKING (HINGE)

The sprint series is the only series that is not named in the play calling of the *Multiple-Motion I Offense*. We use the teen series (14-15, 18-19) to designate the sprint series blocking, the reason being to pare the play names.

The sprint series is really the foundation of the total offensive package. Chapter 7 goes into depth about the coaching of the sprint series and its role in developing offensive consistency for the *Multiple-Motion I Offense*. The sprint draw (14-15) is the key play in the sprint series. The following rules apply to the linemen when blocking the 14-15:

ONSIDE TACKLE: Block 2.
ONSIDE GUARD: Block 1.
CENTER: O; or offside.
OFFSIDE GUARD: Block 1 if over or outside; otherwise block 2.
OFFSIDE TACKLE: Block 2 if over or outside; otherwise block 3.

The crucial block in the sprint draw is the uncovered offensive linemen. For example, in the 5-2 defense, the uncovered linemen would be the guards. They must count 1001, 1002, and show pass while counting and then attack the LB'ers with intelligence. We say intelligence because it doesn't do any good to knock the LB'er down because the sprint draw is a slow developing play and a LB'er on the ground can

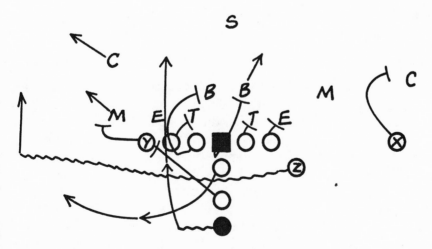

Diagram 2-26: Black-Left 115

get up and still make the tackle. We want our uncovered linemen to screen block the LB'er—breakdown prior to meeting the LB'er in his pass zone responsibility and mirror his actions. Make the LB'er develop width (creating more of a running lane) by attempting to go around you. Once the LB'er takes a side, drive block with rip technique. This block is extremely difficult in the open field, but our feeling is that it will buy time which is more important than knocking the LB'er down immediately.

Even defenses such as the 4-4 and 6-1 make the center the uncovered linemen for the "If" rule—If your man is not over or outside of you, block next man up. (See Diagrams 2-26 and 2-27.)

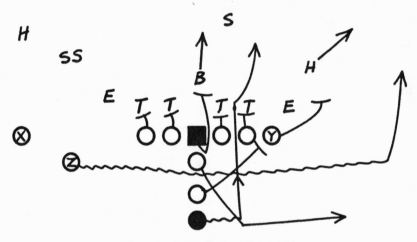

Diagram 2-27: Twins-Right 214

(Hinge)

The hinge block is used for the offside lineman. Whereas the onside lineman blocks aggressively with drive blocks when covered with a down lineman, the hinge block is designed to invite the defensive man to the outside of the offensive lineman. The offside lineman must retreat 2-3 steps from the LOS. The 14-15 sprint-draw must appear as a pass play. The first step back should be the leg opposite of the hand down. This movement still keeps the offensive lineman square which is paramount in good blocking fundamentals. The next step should be the opposite leg with another shuffle step from the original leg. These movements should be coordinated in direct line to the QB's sprint-out route. To keep the lineman in proper alignment with their hinge block, we use a common phrase that is used among many line coaches, "Pretend that you have a camera on your back and you must keep the QB in view."

The hinge block is relatively easy. The hinge block, however, is difficult when blocking a down-lineman if one idea is not stressed— always expect the worst. This expression is stressed constantly to our linemen. The worst to expect on a hinge block is a defensive man slanting hard inside and the offensive lineman cannot recover in time because his first step was too long. We don't give our linemen feet or inches on that first step. We give them slants in practice to block and the individual lineman then begins to understand how far he can go with his first step without losing blocking control on his man. The hinge block, when properly executed, is an extension of the rip technique.

The sprint-draw is a slow developing play. Because of the slow development, the hinge block on the backside is crucial. Most offensive tackles against a 5-2 defensive tackle have a relatively easy hinge block on the backside unless there is a hard inside slant. However, if the backside tackle doesn't block his man longer than normal, the tailback can be tackled before getting untracked. Because the hinge block invites the defensive tackle to the offensive tackle's outside lane, there should be little difficulty if the offensive tackle is aware of the sprint-draw development.

A center's block in the sprint series against a nose guard should be relatively easy if certain fundamentals are understood. The center only has to let the nose guard pick a side and drive block the nose guard sideways. Let the nose guard take himself out. The center can afford this luxury because the tailback will be getting the ball 5-6 yards deep and will have a good 1.5 seconds to view the defensive line, especially his first key—the nose guard's path.

The 18-19 sprint-out run by the QB is the sequential play to the sprint-draw. The blocking rules for the linemen are:

ONSIDE TACKLE:	Block 2.
ONSIDE GUARD:	Block 1.
CENTER:	O; offside.
OFFSIDE GUARD:	Block 1 if over or outside; otherwise block 2.
OFFSIDE TACKLE:	Block 2 if over or outside; otherwise block 3.

The key understanding here for the linemen is that the QB's action will appear as if a sprint-draw or sprint-pass is taking place. The offensive lineman will have the advantage in his drive block on the defensive man. For example, the toss play is a quick read for the defense and requires a reach block because a drive block would not seal off the defensive pursuit. But in the sprint-out by the QB, the defensive line charge should be at such a poor pursuit angle that the drive block with the rip technique will provide a good seal against a defensive line pursuit. (See Diagrams 2-28 and 2-29.)

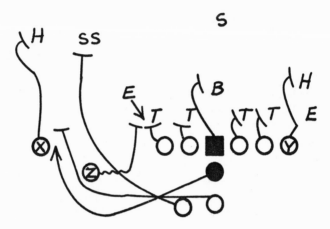

Diagram 2-28: Far-Twins Right 219

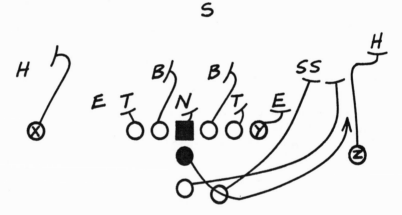

Diagram 2-29: Near-Right 18

VEER BLOCKING

The veer blocking scheme is used as a change-up in our total blocking scheme. We don't run a true veer attack in that the total offensive time is spent on "reading," fullback-QB mesh, pitch relationship, etc. But we do give the linemen veer blocking rules to complement the predetermined veer running plays and implement them into organized practices.

(32-33 Veer)

ONSIDE TACKLE:	First man inside, on or off the LOS.
ONSIDE GUARD:	1.
CENTER:	Onside Gap.
OFFSIDE GUARD:	Onside Gap.
OFFSIDE TACKLE:	Onside Gap.

(34-35, 38-39 Veer)

ONSIDE TACKLE:	2.
ONSIDE GUARD:	1 (pull if you have to).
CENTER:	0; offside.
OFFSIDE GUARD:	"If."
OFFSIDE TACKLE:	"If."

The reason for using the veer is to keep the defense guessing. Our veer is predetermined. Therefore, the *Multiple-Motion I Offense* is not interested in spending time on the "read" factor of the veer. But do we want the defense to spend time on it.

Utilization of the veer blocking scheme is kept simple. If we have success with the veer, naturally we'll keep using it. But the main objective in using the veer is to give that onside LB'er an experience of three men coming down on him; defensive tackle being double-teamed, then left alone on the same offensive look; defensive end being conscious of QB option, then blocked out on the sprint-draw. These happenings help to keep the defense guessing and predictable—which is the concept of the *Multiple-Motion I Offense*.

Diagrams 2-30 and 2-31 illustrate veer running plays against various defenses. Since the veer plays are predetermined as to where the play is going, the analysis of each play will be limited to the blocking schemes as they relate to each play.

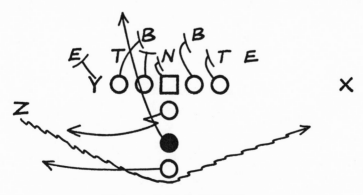

Diagram 2-30: Left 233 Veer

Diagram 2-30 illustrates the 32 Veer against a 5-2 Defense. The center angles toward playside gap with one aim in mind—to seal off the nose guard. The onside guard blocks onside LB'er (No. 1 man). The onside tackle releases inside of the defensive tackle and also blocks the onside LBer.

In Diagram 2-31, if the onside tackle has any difficulty in coming down inside because of the defensive tackle's inside charge, we tell the tackle to go around the defensive tackle. Many times this maneuver creates a wider running lane for the inside veer because the defensive tackle steps out with the onside tackle.

Diagram 2-31: Pinching Def. Tackle

If we are facing a really tough LBer, we sometimes add the word "Ted" to the veer play. This means that the tight end also blocks the LB'er. These maneuvers are only on the inside 32-33 Veer. (See Diagram 2-32.)

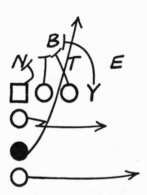

Diagram 2-32: Right-32 Veer-Ted Blocking

Diagram 2-33 illustrates the inside veer against a 6-1 Defense. Again the center has playside gap but must block middle LB'er instead of a nose guard as in the 5-2 Defense. The center must be prepared though for a collision on the LOS if the defensive tackle (No. 1 man) pinches or slants in. If this occurred, the slanting of the No. 1 man, there would be three offensive men blocking him. For the onside guard and tackle block

No. 1 man also. Obviously if this defensive maneuver happened, the inside veer would be doomed on this play. The purpose, however, in showing Diagram 2-33, is to illustrate veer blocking rules, not veer stragety.

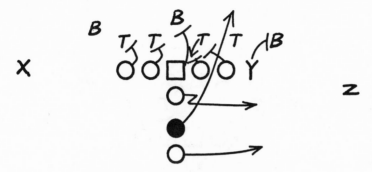

Diagram 2-33: Right-32 Veer

When blocking the outside 34-35 Veer, as shown in Diagram 2-34, the tight-end (Y) and onside tackle always double-team the 2 man unless the 3 man is inside the tight-end, then the tight-end must block the 3 man. If the 2 man disappears inside of the onside tackle, we instruct the tight-ends to continue inside on the onside LB'er as shown in Diagram 2-35.

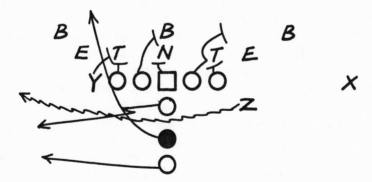

Diagram 2-34: Black-Left 135 Veer

Diagram 2-35: Y Blocking LB'er on 34 Veer

The 38-39 Veer are our predetermined pitch plays which are base blocking assignments without any new adjustments along the LOS by the linemen. The backfield adjustments of the veer are covered in Chapter 5. (See Diagram 2-36.)

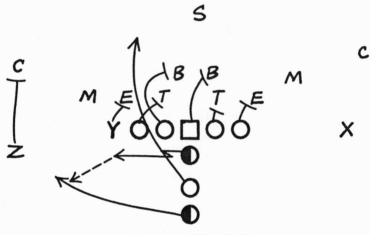

Diagram 2-36: Left 39

WEDGE BLOCKING (GAP)

Wedge blocking is shoulder-to-shoulder blocking. The blockers may wedge over a man or over an open area in the defensive line, with all linemen charging simultaneously toward the apex of the wedge. It is important for all linemen to step with their inside foot. (Splits for wedge blocking should be foot-to-foot.) Shoulder contact is made slightly about the thigh, and moves up into the chest area as contact continues. The linemen maintain shoulder-to-shoulder contact as long as possible wedging the defenders upfield, and the ball carrier selects his hole as it opens.

Wedge blocking is the only blocking scheme that we call at the LOS. The signal for wedge blocking is when any of our interior linemen shout "Gap." The gap call automatically cancels any other blocking scheme that may have been called in the huddle. Moreover, if we sense that a team is going to blitz or show a goal-line defense on a certain situation, we add gap to our play called to insure against inside pressure. For example, if a 22-23 lead would be desired in a short yardage situation, we would add gap to our call, automatically telling the offensive linemen that gap blocking would be utilized instead of lead blocking. (See Diagram 2-37.)

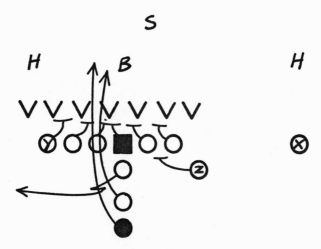

Diagram 2-37: Black-Left 23 Lead

3

Multiple-Motion I
Pass Blocking

Pass-blocking schemes in the *Multiple-Motion I Offense* are broken down into four categories: 60, 70, 80, and screen. The linemen know that it is a pass play when they hear 60, 70, 80, and green (play-action plays with 60 and 80 technique) in the huddle. Direction, left or right, which is used on every play doesn't indicate which side of the line is onside or offside. Just as the last digit in the running plays are used in determining the POA, so it is for the pass plays. If any of the pass plays are ending with an even number, the linemen know that the right side is onside and left is offside. Conversely, the same is true for odd numbers.

60 SERIES

The 60 series is a system of quick passes. The receivers run 3-5 step pass routes. The QB employs a three step dropback. The interior-linemen have only one block to remember when 60 is given in the huddle—chop.

The chop block keeps the defensive linemen's arms down. Since you must have this accomplished for the short, quick pass routes, certain fundamentals are stressed in using the chop block in the 60 series. The legs and body are extended fully into defender. The offensive linemen must be in an extended position. This is the only time that coaches should encourage their linemen to have their weight over the balls of their feet. The head must remain low and aimed directly at the outside hip of the defender. Do not try to arch the back or neck, just fire out and make contact. The hands are in tight to the chest. The elbows are out to make a wider target and provide a cushion to land on.

The chop block has come under heavy criticism for allegedly being conducive to knee injuries. In the use of the chop block, we never have seen any real evidence of the chop block being injurious. The defensive man is taught to read the head of the offensive man. Therefore, we feel that the chop block is easy to read and react to. But the defensive man must use his hands to avoid the block, which is our objective—defensive arms down.

Diagram 3-1 is an example of a 60 series pass play.

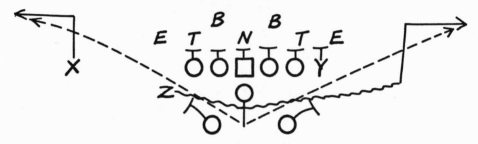

Diagram 3-1: Split-Right 60 Out

The rules for the 60 series are as follows:

ONSIDE GUARD: Block 1.
ONSIDE TACKLE: Block 2.
CENTER: Block 0; offside.
OFFSIDE GUARD: Block 1 if over or outside; otherwise block 2 ("If").
OFFSIDE TACKLE: Block 2 if over or outside; otherwise block 3 ("If").

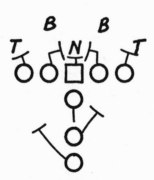

Diagram 3-2: Double-Team Blocking a 60 Pass

There is automatic motion on all 60 passes. This is covered in Chapter 10. If the QB is right-handed, all 60 series plays will make right guard-tackle onside linemen. The opposite if there is a left-handed QB.

If any of the linemen are uncovered, tell them to take a short, inside jab step forward and remain extremely low. When confronting a 5-2 Defense that has an outstanding nose guard, you change up with the guards and have both of them double-team the nose if the guards are uncovered. This insures good protection for the QB in his small passing zone. (See Diagram 3-2.)

DROP-BACK BLOCK
70 SERIES

The 70 series is a drop-back passing attack to complement the sprint-out passing attack. The reason being that a sprint-out passing attack will face secondaries that will rotate their defensive zones to the QB's sprint-out action. The drop-back attack keeps secondaries honest by making them stretch their passing zones the entire width of the total football field. Moreover, the 70 passing series is excellent when desiring optimum pass protection. Besides the five interior linemen, the 70 series employs both backs for pass blocking which can pick up most defensive blitzes.

The techniques of the 70 series blocking are to stay coiled in a break-down position; always keep feet moving; always chop feet in a short, quick step; make the defensive man come to you—don't over extend to hit him; don't commit yourself; use your fist which is in the chin-cheek area to bat defensive man's hands away as he attempts to get to your helmet; make sure your elbows stay in tight to chest just batting from the elbows on up; when you are finally ready to commit yourself, place shoulder in chest or numbers and take the man outside.

There are three common errors in pass blocking:

a. Not moving the feet;
b. Over-extending; and
c. Putting head down or letting man get to the head.

Diagrams 3-3 and 3-4 demonstrate 70 pass series plays.

The blocking rules for the 70 series are as follows:

ONSIDE GUARD:	Inside gap, determines depth.
ONSIDE TACKLE:	Inside gap, determines width.
CENTER:	Block closest inside pressure.

OFFSIDE GUARD: Inside gap; determines depth.
OFFSIDE TACKLE: Inside gap; determines width.
The following are reminders for 70 series blocking:

a. Always guard the inside gap;
b. Defensive man should never get inside;
c. Always force defensive man to outside gap;
d. Guard determines the depth of the pocket; the tackle determines the width;
e. On snap of the ball, the guard takes a short 45 degree angle step back toward the center or to the inside; then he pivots outside foot back, always staying low in good hitting position; and
f. Tackle makes same step as guard except he must take a longer step and must close down a longer distance. He must take a couple of steps. He will also be concentrating on the inside gap, and he will force all defensive players to his outside.

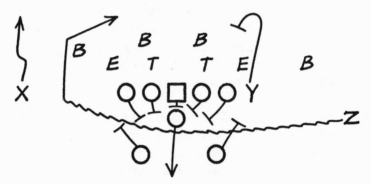

Diagram 3-3: Split-Right 171

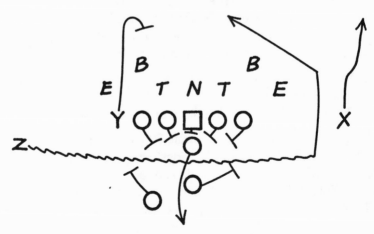

Diagram 3-4: Near-Left 272

The 70 series blocking rules are simple to learn and execute. If the five interior-linemen block their inside gap with zone thinking, stunts and blitzes should be walled off to give the QB a pocket to pass from. Moreover, the two backs help to extend the cup from offensive tackles out. (See Diagram 3-5.)

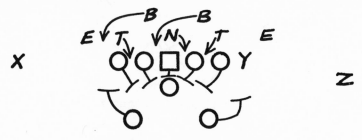

Diagram 3-5: Blocking Stunts

SPRINT-OUT
80 SERIES

The 80 series is the most prevalent pass blocking scheme because of the commitment to the sprint-out attack. The 80 series rules are as follows:

ONSIDE GUARD:	Block 1; if one man drops, help center.
ONSIDE TACKLE:	Block 2 (aggressive drive block).
CENTER:	Block 0; offside.
OFFSIDE GUARD:	Block 1 over or outside; otherwise 2 "If."
OFFSIDE TACKLE:	Block 2 over or outside; otherwise 3 "If."

The fundamentals of the 80 series blocking are very similar to the hinge block technique in Chapter 2. The uncovered linemen on the offside must hinge and react to weakside defensive pressure. The onside linemen block aggressively with down-linemen. If the onside-lineman is uncovered, he blocks down for a double-team.

Block back-door with the offside-linemen who are uncovered. These linemen are taught that their first responsibility is the LB'er, no matter where he goes on a blitz. Once the lineman is convinced that the LB'er is playing his pass responsibility, he pulls back to block weakside pressure. (See Diagram 3-6.)

Diagram 3-6 illustrates the offside guard (right) checking the inside LB'er on a 5-2 Defense. If the LB'er retreats to pass responsibility, the offside guard pulls back to block the defensive end. If the LB'er had blitzed, the offside guard would have been responsible for him. The

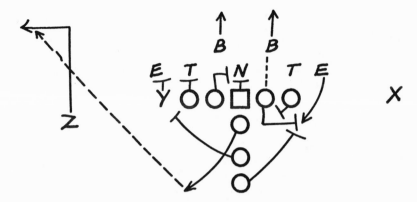

Diagram 3-6: Left 81 Square

defensive end would be picked up by the far back who always blocks backside. The onside guard would check his LB'er (No. 1 man). If he wasn't stunting, the onside guard would double-team the nose guard along the center. The onside tackle blocks (No. 2 man) aggressively. Aggressively means just as he would if the play is a run using the drive block with a rip technique. The reason for blocking aggressively with onside-linemen on down-linemen is to get the defensive line reacting to run and therefore running a pursuit angle for a sprint-out run by the QB instead of a pass rush, for the QB will begin sprint-out action but will stop 5-7 yards deep from the onside tackle's position. (See Diagram 3-7.)

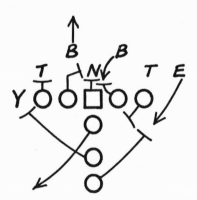

Diagram 3-7: Offside Stunt

In Diagram 3-8, the most dangerous thing that can happen to an offside tackle occurs. This defensive technique against a 5-2 Defense occurs most frequently on the offensive weakside. The reason being that the defensive tackle doesn't have to be concerned about the outside gap since there is no tight-end. The offside tackle must be aware of defenses that are given this opportunity. Moreover, the offside tackle must be drilled repeatedly that his hinge block is nothing if he doesn't protect his inside gap first. To protect himself, the offside tackle must take a short step to his inside first before beginning his hinge technique.

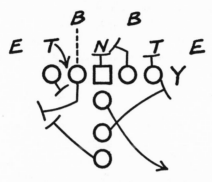

Diagram 3-8: Offside DT Slant

In Diagrams 3-9 and 3-10, the center is the uncovered lineman. In Diagram 3-9, the center blocks weakside pressure after checking the middle LB'er for a stunt. In Diagram 3-10, the center blocks the middle LB'er because he is stunting.

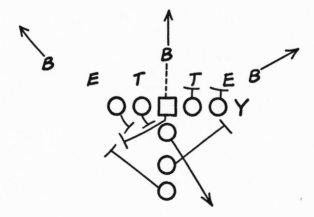

Diagram 3-9: 4-3 Defense

Against a 6-2 Defense, the 80 blocking series can be confusing if the offensive linemen forget their "If" rule. Diagram 3-11 demonstrates the correct 80 technique versus a 6-2 Defense

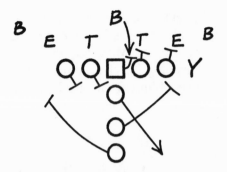

Diagram 3-10: 4-3 Defense (LB'er Stunting)

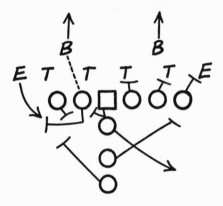

Diagram 3-11: 80 Blocking vs. 6-2

The center blocks the defensive guard because his rule is 0 or offside. Offside guard blocks No. 2 because No. 1 is not over or outside. Therefore, the offside guard is the uncovered lineman and must pull back to block weakside pressure if the No. 2 man (LB'er) is not stunting. The offside tackle blocks No. 3 because his "If" rule also applies; if No. 2 man is not over or outside, block No. 3.

As the uncovered linemen peel back for their back-door block, they must keep these ideas in mind:

1. Block their man under control, keep weight back.
2. Make sure your head is in front (never clip).
3. Block high; if low, defender can jump over you.
4. Don't allow defender to get inside of you and LOS, make defender go around to the outside.

SCREEN BLOCK

The screen block in the *Multiple-Motion I Offense* is an extension of the 80 series. The onside-linemen block their 80 rules, but offside-linemen's rules block screen rules. The offside-linemen in the screen are the screen blockers.

CENTER:	0; offside—2 count; peel man in screen.
OFFSIDE GUARD:	"If"—2 count; form screen.
OFFSIDE TACKLE:	"If"—2 count; form screen.

The screen blockers must be actors. They cannot run out to the screen area immediately. They must count to 2 and block their people on the LOS with convincing technique—but allow defensive men to penetrate. Both the tackle and guard will run 5-7 yards laterally from their interior line positions after counting to 2. The guard and tackle's distance between each other should be at least 5 yards apart. The tackle, as he releases from the LOS, must train himself to look across the field not up the field. For when the split end releases from the LOS, there will be defensive back coverage in the area. This defensive back with a quick key can be in our offensive screen area immediately if the tackle is not prepared to kick him out. (See Diagram 3-13.)

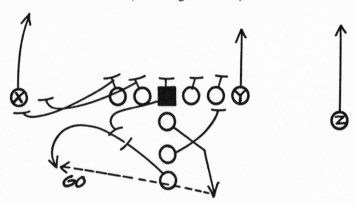

Diagram 3-12: Right 84 Screen Left

The offside guard, when releasing from the LOS, looks for inside pressure from LB'ers. The guard must control his actions to not release from screen area too soon. Once the offensive back receives the ball, he yells "Go!" Only then should the guard begin running upfield for downfield blocking.

Center's block in the screen is a fun block. Why? The center can

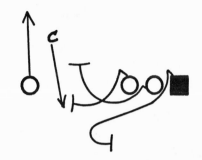

Diagram 3-13: Blocking Cornerback

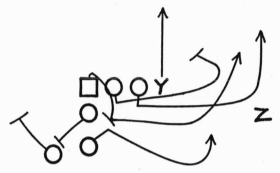

Diagram 3-14: Center's Technique on Screen

escape from the anonymity of the line and block with a sudden surprise on unexpecting defensive linemen who roar into offensive backfield. As the center counts to 2, he begins to peel pack in the offside tackle's area looking for defensive linemen who are running towards the screen. This peel back block is vital to the screen's success. Often during a screen pass, defensive linemen, even though they started out on a pass rush, can catch up to the screen man because the offensive back is standing still waiting for the QB's pass. The center can cut off any inside pressure with his peel back block. But the center has to be careful not to clip. If there is no pressure from the defensive line, the center quickly tries to get in front of the screen pass and block downfield. (See Diagram 3-14.)

4

Quarterbacking the Multiple-Motion I Offense

To be a quarterback in any offensive system, available candidates are judged in three areas: physical attributes, mental abilities, and "heart." Unless you are in a situation where recruiting is permissible for your school system, availability of potential quarterbacks may loom larger than determining who has a stronger arm, better concentration, quicker feet, etc. Offensive football, however, requires an *athlete* for the quarterback position, and regardless whether you have several candidates or one, you as coach must determine that your quarterback can operate with skill.

QUALIFICATIONS

Assuming that your system has the luxury of choosing among several athletes for the quarterback position, physical attributes for the quarterback position in the *Multiple-Motion I Offense* will be discussed first. Ideally, we all want a 6'4", 210 lb., 4.6 40 yd. athlete. But, this kind of athlete is rare and requires much praying to obtain. Most coaches are confronted with a group of athletes that range from 5'7" to 6'2". Speed for the 40 yd. span from 4.8 to 5.3. When confronting the quarterback selection process each year for the *Multiple-Motion I Offense*, a coach must look for three physical qualities: strength of passing arm, foot quickness, and hand size.

The ability to throw the ball from at least medium length (40 yds.) to great length (50 or more yds.) is the first prerequisite. Accuracy or slow release of the football are unimportant because they can be taught. However, the ability to pass a football far cannot be taught. This ability to be able to pass at least 40 yds. is a must for the offense to be multiple when attacking defenses. If the quarterbacks are unable to throw deep, so many of the sequential plays such as the sprint-draw, screens, and quarterback sprint-outs will bog down due to the lack of vertical depth and horizontal width by the defenses.

Quickness is another ingredient that is necessary for successful quarterback play. Quickness not measured in lightning-timed 40 yd. dashes, but the ability to move hands and feet rapidly in coordinated fashion. Jumping rope is one of the skill tests in helping to select quarterback personnel for quickness. Quickness is paramount in executing the various pivots, hand-offs, and passing pockets. If the quarterback cannot move quickly, the offense will not move quickly. Of course, if this happens, the offense is no longer multiple and is predictable to defense.

Hand size is vital for proper hand-offs and successful passing. Normally, height is directly related to hand size. But if you have a young man who can pass and is quick, hand size becomes less important, unless he can only pass by continually gripping the ball before passing. If this occurs, your chances of coaching your quarterback to release the ball quickly and executing pivots with clean hand-offs diminish. Proper hand size can be determined if your quarterback can pick up the football with one hand and drop it and still be able to catch it with the same hand.

The mental abilities of the quarterback position in the *Multiple-Motion I Offense* can be broken down into intelligence and concentration.

Concentration is more important if both areas are equal. For example, if you have an athlete who has an I.Q. of 140 but cannot concentrate when executing the multiplicity of offensive football, your quarterback's I.Q. of 140 might as well be 40. Concentration is closely related to attitude. The quarterback's perspective on football and his own personal goals can deter or reinforce his concentration in executing offensive plays. Because of the many outside factors that can interrupt a young man's struggle in becoming a quarterback, "heart" becomes the determining factor.

"Heart" is desire, moxy, knowing how to win, perseverance—an unwillingness to concede defeat. Whatever description might mean "heart," a good quarterback has it. It cannot be coached or taught. It is there. Only the coach must be able to see it and nurture it. "Heart" in any sport or position is a factor that cannot be categorized, but yet—not overlooked. Bill Kilmer of the Washington Redskins was able to continue to play professional football even though his physical talents had waned in his later years. Why? He had "heart."

There are many ways in which coaches try to gauge their quarterbacks for that intensity to be a winner. Some coaches keep rotating their quarterback candidates until pressure pares the candidates down to one. Others put the quarterbacks through rigorous practice sessions—mental and physical—hoping that the "cream rises to the top." Whatever method chosen, a quarterback in the *Multiple-Motion I Offense* must have "heart" to be successful.

LEAD TECHNIQUE

The quarterback's primary concern in executing the 22-23 Lead is to get the ball as deep as possible to the tailback so that he has more time to read the POA. As the quarterback receives the snap, he quickly pivots in the direction of the lead play. If, for example, a 23 Lead is called, the quarterback would push off his right inside foot and pivot to his left so that his left foot would be almost behind the right foot. (Diagram 4-1.)

From this point on, the quarterback would run to the tailback carrying the football with two hands and placing the football into the tailback's stomach. After the handoff, the quarterback should continue running around the end.

Diagram 4-1: Lead Technique

(AS DEEP AS POSSIBLE)

COUNTER TECHNIQUE

The quarterback in running the 40-41 Counter must be quick on his feet and yet display good faking. If the play is the 40 Counter, the quarterback would pivot just as he did in the 22-23 Lead. However, the quarterback pivots opposite of the hole called and must fake to the fullback before handing-off to the tailback. (Diagram 4-2.)

Diagram 4-2: Counter Technique

Coaching points to be aware of:

1. First step must be behind opposite foot or collision with fullback could occur. Moreover, trail leg on first step must come up quickly to protect against deep penetration which could trip the quarterback.
2. Quarterback must carry ball with two hands and only motion with the ball to the fullback passing by, do not put the ball in fullback's arms.
3. Quarterback must strive for depth in getting the ball to the tailback so as to give the tailback more time to read the POA.
4. When faking with the ball, keep arms bent and above the waist so that the fullback's knees cannot jar ball loose.
5. Do not look back after handing-off, but continue on fake run around end.

TRAP TECHNIQUE

The 30-31 Trap is a most difficult maneuver for the quarterback when using the I formation. The reason is the closeness of the quarterback and fullback. The quarterback must get the ball deep to the fullback so he can read the trap guard's block. The problem though is that the quarterback has to pivot correctly and quickly to insure a clean hand-off.

If a 31 Trap is called, the quarterback knows that he will pivot the opposite direction. First, he will again push-off the opposite foot with inside pressure and bring his pivot leg behind with as much depth as possible. The trail leg should be moved as quickly as possible behind the pivot leg. With this second step, the hand-off between quarterback and fullback should occur. The quarterback continues fake opposite of pivot step. (See Diagram 4-3.)

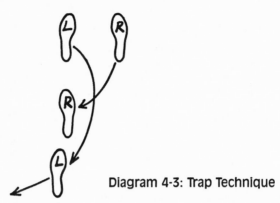

Diagram 4-3: Trap Technique

TOSS TECHNIQUE

The 26-27 Toss is the same pivot as the Trap except the quarterback tosses the ball instead of handing-off when completing the second step. The quarterback tosses the ball with two hands and the ball rotation should be end-over-end.

Coaching points to be aware of:

1. Quarterback must step back, not sideways, to insure clearance from fullback's path if in I formation (can run toss out of near or far backfield formations which reduces possibility of hitting other backs with the football).
2. Quarterback's arms must follow through to point aimed at— back's stomach. If arms go above this point, ball is usually too high to handle.
3. Quarterback must run between onside guard and tackle to help with sealing off defensive pursuit. (Don't get real brave.)
4. Don't rush snap, or else fumble will occur. Quickness is vital but not haste.

SPRINT-OUT TECHNIQUE

The sprint-out technique entails two different maneuvers. But, both the 14-15 and 18-19 do require one similar maneuver to initiate them—quarterback must sprint from the center at a 45° angle every time.

The 14-15 is our sprint-draw and requires great timing between the quarterback and tailback to insure success. The quarterback upon receiving the snap, sprints to a 45° angle with eyes upfield and ball in a passing position. The quarterback's first two steps should be in this pattern. After third step, the quarterback now brings his attention to the mesh point—5-7 yds. behind onside tackle. Without lowering arms below the waist, the quarterback hands-off inside with both hands on the ball. After the hand-off, the quarterback continues to fake around end. (See Diagram 4-4.)

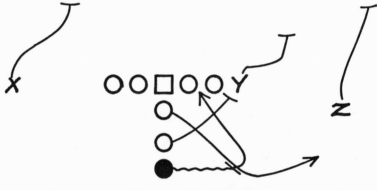

Diagram 4-4: Right 14

The 18-19 is the only pure run (no option) by the quarterback in the *Multiple-Motion I Offense*. Again, the quarterback sprints out to side called with 45° angle step. But this time, both backs block and the quarterback runs to sprint area (5-7 yds. behind onside tackle), without any faking. As the quarterback sprints back, his eyes are downfield and the ball up in a passing position with both hands. Once the quarterback

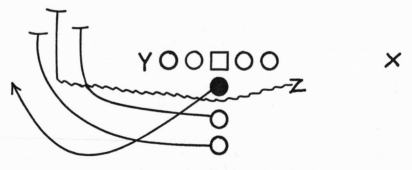

Diagram 4-5: Black-Left 119

reaches the sprint-out area behind the onside tackle, he begins to run toward the defensive end area reading the fullback's and tailback's block on defensive end. As the quarterback begins his forward movement, he continues to show pass by arm pump fakes. Once near the LOS, the quarterback tucks the football away and runs to daylight. (See Diagram 4-5.)

VEER TECHNIQUE

The veer techniques in the *Multiple-Motion I Offense* are not as detailed as a true veer attack. The quarterback does not read on the veer because every segment of the veer ir predetermined unless the quarterback decides to option the defensive end specifically.

When running the 32-33 Inside Veer, the quarterback takes one step back in a 45° angle toward side of play called. While stepping in this direction, he immediately looks back to the fullback and places the ball with two hands and arms straight into the fullback's stomach. The quarterback, however, doesn't release the ball immediately, but waits until trail leg has become parallel to the pivot leg and the fullback is even with trail leg. Once the quarterback has handed off, he continues down the LOS in parallel fashion and fake pitches to the tailback. (Diagram 4-6.)

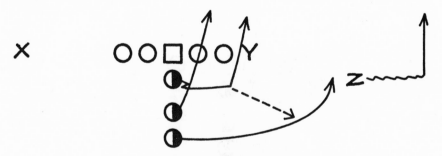

Diagram 4-6: Right 232 Veer

The 34-35 Outside Veer is down the line action by the quarterback. Again he places both hands on the ball and holds the ball chest high when running down the LOS. The mesh point is behind the inside leg of the onside tackle. There the quarterback looks ball into the fullback's stomach and rides the ball until the fullback is even with the quarterback's leg closest to LOS. After handing-off, the quarterback continues down the line and carries out fake pitch to the tailback. (See Diagram 4-7.)

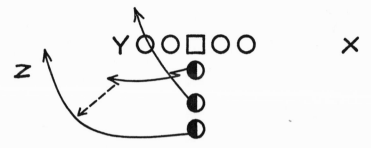

Diagram 4-7: Left 35 Veer

The 38-39 Veer is a predetermined pitch. This play requires several techniques by the quarterback. First the quarterback's mesh-point with the fullback is as if a 32-33 Veer was called. But this time the quarterback brings football back to chest area after riding fullback with the football. The quarterback runs parallel down the LOS reading the defensive end. If the quarterback cannot see the defensive end's numbers, the quarterback fakes a pitch showing football, then tucks ball away and runs inside of defensive end. However, if the defensive end's numbers can be seen, the quarterback pitches to tailback because the end must try to turn back, and it is virtually impossible to catch a tailback who is running full speed when receiving ball. (See Diagram 4-8.)

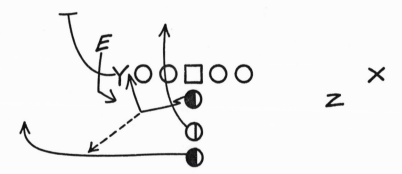

Diagram 4-8: Pre-determined Option 38-39

A change-up in attacking the defensive end is the speed option. This entails both backs running parallel along the LOS with the fullback blocking outside of defensive end area. The quarterback initiates the play with "Alabama action." Alabama action means the quarterback retreats from center snap moving in back pedal fashion (2-3 yds.) clutching the football with two hands near the chest area. This maneuver is designed to get the LB'ers moving back to pass zone areas. After the quarterback plants feet, he pushes off with offside foot and runs right at defensive end. If the defensive end comes up, the quarterback pitches to the tailback. Otherwise, the quarterback runs inside of the defensive end. (See Diagram 4-9.)

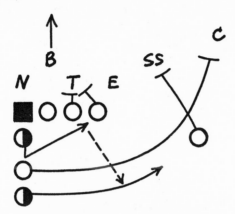

Diagram 4-9: Speed Option

PASSING GAME TECHNIQUE

The 60 Passing Series is a timing series. The quarterback must get the exchange from the center, position ball in throwing position, set up in three steps, and release the ball to receiver immediately upon pivot. The three steps from the center exchange are vital to the quarterback's success on the 60 series. The quarterback must step back first with the leg that is on the side of his passing arm. The second step is with the opposite leg. The third step is with the passing leg, and the quarterback is ready to push-off with his passing side in correct follow-through. If the quarterback doesn't initiate his three step drop with his passing leg, the timing of the 60 series will be doomed. Although the 60 series is not a deep threat, all patterns are either three, four, or five step routes, this series requires more athletic ability and technique than any other passing series in the *Multiple-Motion I Offense.*

If there is proper execution between the quarterback and receiver, the 60 series patterns should be completed within 2.5 seconds. The quarterback must be able to drop back directly behind the center and plant back foot and fire in three steps. Only the split-end (X) and flanker (Z) run the 60 series. Therefore, the quarterback is asked to "look off" one receiver and pass to the other. This requirement means the quarterback has to utilize great technique in completing the pass.

Because the 60 series is designed for two receivers only, you ask your quarterback to throw to the receiver who has the least coverage. If confronted with a four deep secondary, throw away from the strong-side safety. If a three deep secondary, the quarterback passes away from the monster or rover-back. Since secondary coverages can be confusing to read for a quarterback when executing such a short-timed passing series as the 60, you throw all your 60 passes with automatic motion from the black formation. (See Diagrams 4-10 and 4-11.)

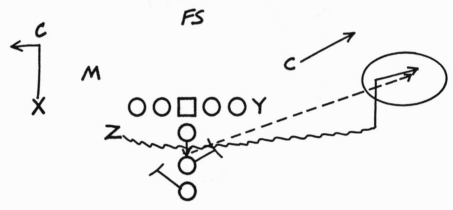

Diagram 4-10: Right 60 Out (Automatic Black Formation)

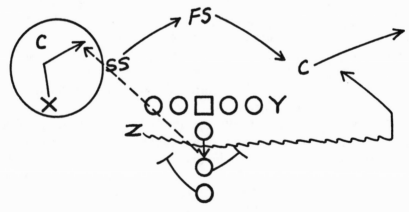

Diagram 4-11: Right 60 Slant

The philosophy on the 60 Series is to throw under the coverage. This helps to serve as a sequential series to the deeper passing patterns because the secondary is lulled into thinking that short patterns are being run. Because you want to throw under the deep coverage, you want your 60 Passes to be safe from interceptions. Therefore, the quarterbacks are always reading where the two-man zone coverage is being utilized. There are very few high schools that utilize a three-man rushing defense and four short, three deep passing zone. Most schools utilize the conventional four deep and three deep secondary philosophy. As long as this trend continues, you will continue to pass the 60 Series utilizing motion to distinguish where the two-man zone coverage can be found.

70 SERIES TECHNIQUE

The 70 Series is a drop-back passing series. In this series, three receivers are utilized: tight-end (Y), split-end (X), and flanker (Z). The 70 Series has maximum protection with five interior linemen and two backs blocking. The quarterback sets up from 5-7 yds, directly behind the center. A good time for this drop-back set up should range from 1.8 to 1.4 seconds. As the quarterback receives the snap, the ball should be brought up immediately to shoulder level with both hands on the ball and the passing hand placed on the seam where he will pass the ball. Simultaneously, the quarterback retreats in backward fashion using a crossover step. The shoulder carriage should be relaxed and move freely as the legs retreat backwards. Depth is only determined by a "sixth sense" which is nurtured during continuous passing drills. The quarterback shouldn't have to count steps to get proper depth. He has enough to worry about. Once the quarterback gets his proper depth, he should keep the ball shoulder high with most of his weight on the back foot. From this point the quarterback scans the field using any movement that he feels comfortable with. Many quarterback coaches insist on a foot shuffle, jumping in place, very little movement. etc. *This is over-coaching.* The quarterback's athletic ability should dictate from this point on, not a quarterback coach's philosophy that worked for him.

The 70 Series patterns will be discussed in detail in Chapter 6. Nonetheless, the quarterback will always have three receivers involved in his patterns. These patterns will vary according to who the primary receiver will be. For example, if (Y) is the primary receiver, (X) and (Z) will run predetermined routes which are automatically known to the quarterback and receivers. The execution of the 70 Series pass plays by the quarterback are determined by his success to read the onside LB'er. Always consider the LB'er who is on (Y's) side to be the onside LB'er.

As the ball is centered, the quarterback retreats for the required depth, and reads the movements of the onside LB'er. If the LB'er stunts, the quarterback will pass the ball to the tight-end who is the "hot receiver." (See Diagrams 4-12, 4-13, and 4-14.)

If (Y) is the primary receiver, the quarterback will read the movements of the onside LB'er and hopefully establish a passing lane for (Y) with (Y's) cooperation and understanding of LB'er's defensive pass movement. (See Diagrams 4-15 and 4-16.)

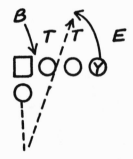

Diagram 4-12: Reading Hot Receiver

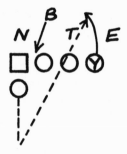

Diagram 4-13: Reading Hot Receiver

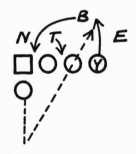

Diagram 4-14: Reading Hot Receiver

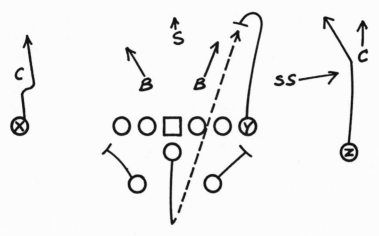

Diagram 4-15: Y Primary Receiver

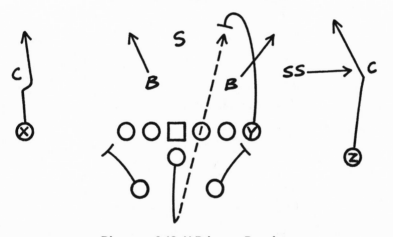

Diagram 4-16: Y Primary Receiver

However, if (Y) is the secondary receiver, he will only be utilized for safety pass if onside LB'er goes. When (Z) is running his post, the quarterback looks immediately at free safety area for defensive weakness. (X's) automatic pattern, the UP, is strictly a throw-away pass keeping the defense honest. The quarterback, however, always passes the ball to the outside shoulder when passing an UP pattern so that the free safety's play cannot be involved. (See Diagrams 4-17 and 4-18)

With the 70 Series having a multitude of different pass patterns, the quarterback's keys seem so endless that confusion could be reinforced instead of execution. But, the quarterback has only *two* keys. Read onside LB'er and then pick up the primary receiver immediately and execute. The coaches are responsible for dissecting the defensive second-ary's weaknesses with their eagle-eye view from the press box. All that is expected from the quarterback is for him to read the onside LB'er and then pass to the primary receiver, giving the primary receiver time to run his route properly. If the primary receiver's route is a poor call, the quarterback should be aware of when and where to throw the ball away.

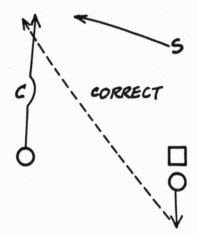

Diagram 4-17: Correct Up Pattern

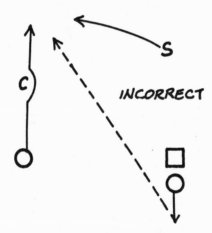

Diagram 4-18: Incorrect Up Pattern

80 SERIES TECHNIQUE

The 80 Series is another feature of the sprint passing series. Whereas the quarterback runs or passes on his sprint-out with Green

18-19, in the 80 Series the quarterback sets up behind the onside tackle. The set up by the quarterback does not restrict his option to run, but only his running and passing lane which the Green 18-19 develops.

The quarterback sprints at a 45° angle to a 5-7 yd. area behind the onside tackle. Regardless of how the quarterback passes the ball, he must look downfield all the time (to see any blitzing LB'er) as he releases from the LOS. In addition to his downfield look, the quarterback must carry the ball at shoulder level with both hands on the ball. You do not want the quarterback to have to wind up in order to release the ball.

The quarterback's technique in releasing the ball while in motion is vital for success. The quarterback has to get his shoulder and hips rotated to get proper passing form. Use the expression "belly button downfield." If the quarterback doesn't rotate his shoulders and hips forward, the ball will be released across the body which will result in poor velocity and accuracy. The quarterback must be able to throw off either foot when passing on the run, because when the receiver is open, the ball has to be delivered. If not, and the quarterback waits to get his best foot positioned to throw, the receiver may be already covered.

The reads on the Green 18-19 Series are determined by the secondary's reaction to our use of motion. Chapter 7 gives detailed comments on how to implement the sprint-out passing attack against various secondary coverages.

The 80 Series, however, utilizes the same reads or keys as the 70 Series. There are three different pass plays in the 80 Series: 81-82, 83-84, and 83-84 Flood.

The 81-82 pass play requires no key on the onside LB'er because (Y) is not involved in the pass pattern, but remains on the LOS to block. The 81-82 pass play is a sprint-out by the quarterback using the 80 Series technique and passing to one receiver running the route called (Example 82 Curl). The secondary receiver runs a crossing pattern which is detailed in Chapter 6. The crossing pattern always compliments the primary receiver in the 81-82 pass play. The quarterback may call any individual route off the passing tree for the 81-82 pass play. Regardless of the direction called by the quarterback in giving the play in the huddle, the quarterback always sprints to the side of the last digit called which indicates onside. (See Diagrams 4-19 and 4-20.)

In Diagram 4-19 and 4-20 there is not a hot receiver because Y remains in to block. Therefore, with no "hot" read key, the quarterback keys his primary receiver immediately. If defensive pressure comes from within because of a stunt, the quarterback attempts to pass the ball away or eats the ball.

The 83-84 pass play requires two keys for the quarterback. One is the onside LB'er near (Y) and the second key is the strong safety or monster's drop in the short zone to the onside. (See Diagram 4-21.)

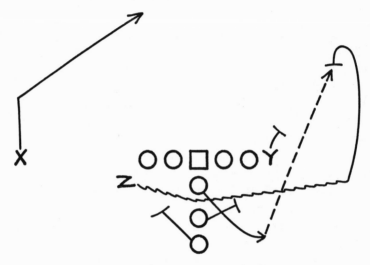

Diagram 4-19: Black-Right 282 Hook

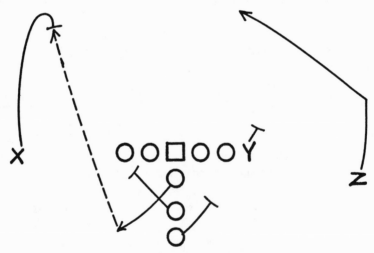

Diagram 4-20: Right 81 Hook

The quarterback reads onside LB'er to (Y's) side to see if he blitzes. If the LB'er does vacate, the quarterback passes the ball to (Y) who is the "hot receiver." However, if onside LB'er drops to hook zone, the

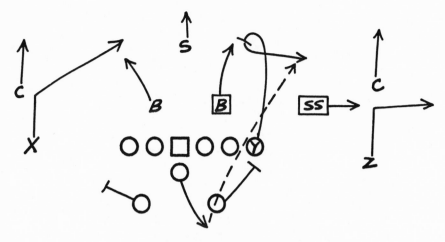

Diagram 4-21: 84 Pass

quarterback reads the seam between (Y) and the LB'er. This seam is the throwing lane for the quarterback and requires separation between (Y) and the onside LB'er. (Y) slides to the outside after hooking to separate from the LB'er. As (Y) moves to the outside, only the strong safety can prevent a good seam from developing. If this occurs, the strong safety floating to the inside, the quarterback passes the ball to the flanker on the out pattern. (See Diagram 4-22.)

(X) runs a deep post to keep the free safety involved and out of the area where the tight-end is hooking. Naturally, if the free safety is coming up too quickly, the quarterback should be instructed to throw the deep post. The quarterback, however, should not be responsible for diagnosing this, the coaches are.

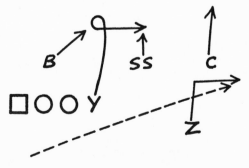

Diagram 4-22: 84 Pass

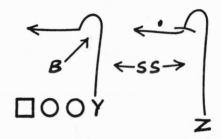

Diagram 4-23: 84 Flood Pass

The 83-84 Flood is the triple hook by all three receivers and a flat route by the near back. Because the 83-84 Flood calls for a flat route by a back, this play always requires a near or far formation to enable a quick release for the back to enter the flat area. The quarterback's keys are again the onside LB'er near (Y) and the strong safety. But (Y) doesn't slide this time to the outside, but to the inside. (See Diagram 4-23.)

The quarterback reads onside LB'er and looks for a blitz, then seam development from (Y). If the seam doesn't appear quickly, the quarterback looks to (Z) immediately and reads strong safety's position. If the strong safety slides to the outside, (Z) will move inside on hook and should be open. If the strong safety remains inside of (Z) on his hook, the quarterback knows that the flat pass to the outside will be available to the back coming out of the backfield. (See Diagrams 4-24 and 4-25.)

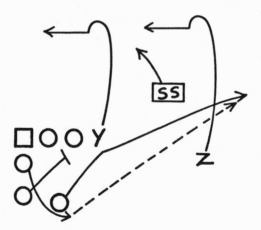

Diagram 4-24: 84 Flood

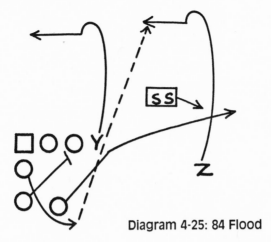

Diagram 4-25: 84 Flood

SCREEN SERIES TECHNIQUE

The screen series utilized in the *Multiple-Motion I Offense* is sequenced from out of 80 Series technique. The quarterback sprints to his normal passing area at a 45° angle. Upon setting up, the quarterback then begins his retreat. However, the quarterback must set up just as he normally does or else the defense will read the screen quickly. On the quarterback's retreat from his passing zone, he maintains his "downfield look." When the running back is in the screen area, the quarterback plants and releases the ball. Naturally, if the pass rush is so fierce that planting and throwing would be impossible, the quarterback must lob the ball while back-pedaling. But this maneuver is not what is usually desired when running the screen play. The screen play by the quarterback should be where he can release the ball strong and quickly. If the screen man is ever covered, the quarterbacks are taught to run at the screen man. When the screen man recognizes that the quarterback has discarded the screen, he begins to run downfield. The quarterback continues to run in the screen area and attempts to dump the ball to the screen man running downfield or run for daylight. The quarterback must always remember that his dump pass should not be a desperation heave. Only pass the ball if the screen man is open. Losing yardage can happen on any play, but losing the ball in a panic-stricken moment is unpardonable and psychologically damaging to the football team. If the quarterback panics, the offensive team has no leader.

5

Multiple-Motion I Backfield Techniques

PHYSICAL AND MENTAL QUALIFICATIONS

The *Multiple-Motion I Offense* implements two running backs on most of its runs with the exceptions being the quarterback on sprint runs and the flanker (Z) on special draws and reverses (Chapter 10). The physical attributes desired for these two positions—fullback, tailback—can cover a myriad of superman qualities, But, in reality, there are two physical traits that should be uppermost in selecting personnel for these positions.

The fullback must have size then quickness, if possible. Since the fullback position requires blocking on a large percentage of the plays, the fullback position is much like that of an offensive guard. He must be able to block well or the offense will sputter. Moreover, the fullback's blocks are normally one-on-one situations at critical gaps in the POA. If the fullback has size with his quickness, then running plays designed for the fullback can be used more frequently. But, the crucial factor in selecting a fullback is his ability to block large defensive tackles efficiently as well as slippery cornerbacks. Quickness in the fullback position is a plus and adds more diversity in the offense. But, if the fullback is not quick, he can still block because of the fullback's alignment in the I formation (3½ yards from ball).

The tailback's position requires the reverse of the fullback's desired physical attributes. The tailback position must have quickness. Size is no factor unless the tailback has both speed and size, then the tailback position becomes even more potent. The quickness factor cannot be overlooked. Since the tailback will receive the ball from 5-7 yards from the LOS, he must be able to accelerate to the POA before the opening closes. Tailbacks who have quickness and a tremendous desire to be the best are going to be great regardless if they weigh 140 lbs. or 210 lbs. John McKay, former head football coach at U.S.C. an acknowledged authority on the I formation, has been quoted many times on the utilization of the tailback in the I. McKay stresses patience in running the tailback. If you know as a coach what kind of physical and mental qualities the starting tailback has, the end results will be positive if you have patience in running the ball 20-25 times with the tailback.

Undoubtedly, mental qualities of the running backs will determine the offensive success. Are your fullback and tailback mentally tough? Can your fullback repeatedly bang heads with the opponent's best defensive player while the tailback does most of the scoring? Will your tailback fatigue mentally when carrying the ball 20-25 times? All of these questions are vital in determining if you will have offensive success. Unselfishness and mental toughness are attitudes that should be displayed and felt in the fullback and tailback positions. You, as the coach, must cultivate these attitudes to a positive self-image for the players' relationship to other team members.

STANCE AND HAND-OFFS

The fullback is always in a 3 pt. stance. Many football teams have their fullback in a 4 pt. stance to insure greater quickness when going forward. The *Multiple-Motion I Offense,* however, requires quickness laterally as well as forward. Therefore, coach the fullbacks to be in a 3 pt. stance so lateral quickness will be less handicapped. If the backfield formation is base, the tailback will be in a 2 pt. stance. This is the only time that any of the running backs are in a 2 pt. stance. The tailback uses a 3 pt. stance when not operating base. Hand pressure and eye movement can tip off to a defense where the ball is going. The running backs must be balanced in stance and eye movement.

Hand-offs in backfield play can be taken as lightly as the quarterback-center exchange by many coaches. But, if there is a mistake in this simple maneuver, an 80 yard drive can be stopped. Coaches should stress hand-offs in drills and these three factors during a drill period:

1. Inside arm is up and parallel to the ground. Form pocket with bottom arm so that a basketball can be placed in it.
2. As the running back approaches hand-off point with quarter-

back, he must not look at the quarterback or ball but straight ahead to the POA.

3. Once the ball is placed in the pocket, the running back's hands should be cupped over both points of the football. Keep both arms on the football until past LOS. When open, put ball in arm away from tacklers. When there is going to be a collision, put both arms around the football. Fumbles are not only damaging to offensive consistency, but demoralizing for psychological reasons.

RECOGNITION OF POINT-OF-ATTACK (POA)

The numbering system in the *Multiple-Motion I Offense* uses even numbers on the right and odd numbers on the left. These numbers, however, are not always the true indication of where the POA is. The backs should run to where the blocking schemes create the POA. With today's sophisticated defenses, the POA on the same running play could jump from the onside guard hole to the onside tackle hole. The numbering system gives the communication system an understanding, but the blocking schemes create the holes. The running backs must not only understand how the POA will be attacked, but also be able to run to the correct POA. When the running backs do run with the ball, "North-South" style must be encouraged. "North-South" is referring to running the ball in a direct line to the goal-line. A good running back must realize his physical limitations. If you are really an O.J. Simpson type runner, do your thing. But if you are a mere mortal, never dance sideways, but pound that ball forward.

LEAD TECHNIQUE

The lead series almost always employs cross blocking at the POA (unless a 6-2 defense occurs). In this cross-blocking scheme, the onside LB'er will be blocked by an offensive lineman and the fullback. The fullback's technique is simple—block through POA on the onside LB'er. The tailback's technique is simple enough—receive the hand-off and run to daylight. Running to daylight, however, cannot be simplified. The tailback has to be aware of the POA. For example, if a 22 Lead has been called, see Diagrams 5-1, 5-2, 5-3 and 5-4 for the various POA's.

In Diagram 5-1, the tailback, being cognizant of the blocking schemes involved in the 22-23 Lead, runs inside of the onside guard's cross block on the defensive tackle. Whereas, in Diagram 5-2 the tailback runs a wider lane against the 4-4 defensive tackle. The tailback knows that the onside tackle will be caving down the defensive tackle. Diagram 5-3 is a similar path for the tailback against 5-2 Eagle defense. Again he

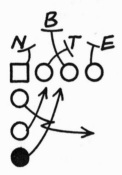

Diagram 5-1

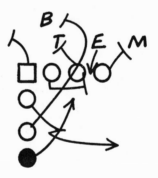

Diagram 5-2

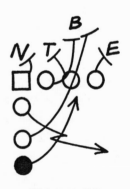

Diagram 5-3

must run outside of the onside tackle's block on the defensive tackle. Diagram 5-4 shows the POA between the onside guard and onside tackle against the 6-2 Defense. The key read here is the fullback's block on the onside LBer. The lead series is not designed for deception. It is the most basic isolation play that I formations utilize. The tailback's key is reading the POA and running for the open seam.

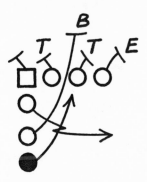

Diagram 5-4

COUNTER TECHNIQUE

The counter series is the sequential play off the lead series. The fullback again has a simple technique. But instead of running through number called, the fullback runs through the opposite number and fakes as if he is carrying the ball. The fullback's main concerns are staying low and trying to get tackled at the LOS. The tailback's technique is to drop-step, plant back foot, and push off toward the POA. The POA on the

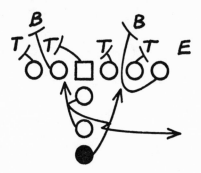

Diagram 5-5: 40 Counter

counter will vary like all of the running plays in the *Multiple-Motion I Offense*. Examples of the counter's POA are shown in Diagrams 5-5 and 5-6.

In Diagram 5-5, the tailback must hit the POA between the onside guard and tackle. Using his drop-step to delay his forward motion, the tailback will key the tight-end (Y) fold blocking through on the onside LB'er. The key is keeping your eyes open and recognizing the defense from the two point stance.

In Diagram 5-6, the tailback runs through the POA at the center and onside guard gap. The key block is the onside tackle fold blocking on the onside LB'er.

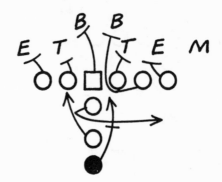

Diagram 5-6: 40 Counter

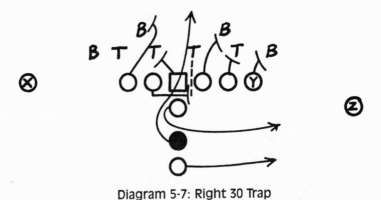

Diagram 5-7: Right 30 Trap

TRAP TECHNIQUE

The trap series can be designed for the fullback and tailback. When base formation (I) is being employed, the trap play is automatically going to the fullback. The fullback's technique is to receive the hand-off opposite from the trap hole called. (See Diagram 5-7.)

Normally, the path run by the fullback will be a snake pattern. This pattern is necessary so that the fullback can read the trapping guard's block. The tailback runs parallel to the LOS in the same direction of trap called. While the tailback is running his parallel path to the LOS, the quarterback is faking an option with him.

If the trap play is called with near or far as backfield formation, the tailback or the fullback can be the ball-carrier. If a third digit is added to the trap play, the flanker will begin motion and the tailback knows he is the ball-carrier. If the trap play is called without motion, the fullback carries the ball. (See Diagrams 5-8 and 5-9.)

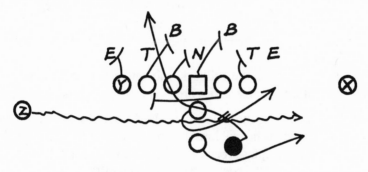

Diagram 5-8: Far-Left 231 Trap

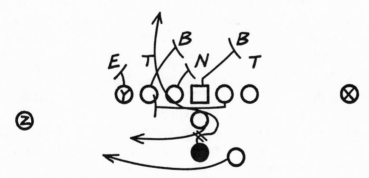

Diagram 5-9: Far-Left 31 Trap

The tailback's assignment on near or far when not carrying the ball on the trap is the same as base trap plays—run parallel to the LOS in the direction of the trap play called faking option with the quarterback. The only change for the fullback and the tailback in the near or far formations is that the fullback goes opposite laterally from the trap play called. The fullback must be consicious of not running into the tailback. To insure preventing this collision, the fullback must drop step and belly back away from the LOS. The tailback's technique on the trap play is always the same—counter step away from the quarterback, plant and push, and receive inside hand-off.

TOSS TECHNIQUE

The toss series is not complicated for the fullback or tailback to execute. Moreover, the toss series can be employed from base, near, or far (if motion is used) formation. If base is being used, the tailback automatically receives the ball and the fullback blocks. Otherwise, the near and far formations enable the fullback to carry the ball with the tailback blocking.

The key points for the fullback and tailback to remember when carrying the ball on the toss series are:

1. Move laterally to the LOS when coming out of stance. If the back moves forward, he will have less reaction time to receive the ball; moreover, the quarterback could pull up on his pitch because of the nearness of the back and deliver a toss that would be difficult to handle.
2. Never take your eyes off the ball. Look ball into your hands.
3. Key other back's block on corner. However, maintain a wide viewing scope when running around corner and accelerate in "North-South" fashion when open seam develops.

Blocking for the toss series requires quickness and a willingness to collide with defensive personnel. The only blocking rule that the near carrying back must know is that he will block the corner or outside force of the defensive perimeter. Normally, this block will require a kick-out block and the ball carrier will run inside of the ball. But, whatever the outside defensive pressure does, the blocking back must come under control, maintain eye contact as long as possible, and get a collision of any kind. Preferably, the running shoulder block is the most desirable. But, if the cornerback is running scared and dancing around, the blocking back must be able to control his forward movement enough so that he can screen out the defender from the ball carrier.

VEER TECHNIQUE

The veer in the *Multiple-Motion I Offense* is predetermined. Therefore, the back's technique on the veer is not as precise as the veer-dominated attack. The inside veer which utilizes the fullback as the ball carrier simply has the fullback running a path toward the outside leg of the onside guard. The tailback runs parallel to the LOS faking the option with the quarterback. On the outside veer, the fullback's path is now changed to the outside leg of the onside tackle. Again, the tailback and the quarterback carry out their option fake. When the predetermined pitch is called, the fullback fakes his inside veer route and then blocks first man to show. The tailback runs his parallel route with the LOS and receives the pitch 5-7 yards from the original tailback position. If the quarterback continues down the line with the ball, the tailback must maintain pitch relationship. This pitch relationship should be at least 5 yards deep and a 45° angle from the quarterback. The tailback should be almost running forward when receiving the pitch.

A key point in discussing the veer in the *Multiple-Motion I Offense* is that the veer is only presented to "appear" as a total veer package so that the defense must spend a lot of practice time stopping it. The veer techniques of a true veer could encompass a whole book. The *Multiple-Motion I Offense* is only intended to show the veer in the multiple philosophy. Moreover, time would not allow the backfield to learn the total veer techniques along with the other features of the *Multiple-Motion I Offense*.

SPRINT SERIES

The sprint series in the *Multiple-Motion I Offense* encompasses more backfield technique than the other running series discussed. Each back can exchange roles on blocking contain if different backfield formations are used. Moreover, when the sprint-draw is employed, specific backfield steps must be employed by the tailback or else all timing is destroyed. These specific techniques must be executed or the offensive attack will sputter.

When running the sprint-out by the quarterback, the backs' rules are this: near back blocks widest man on LOS with sprint block technique; far back sprint blocks 1 yard past near backs' block, help near back if help is needed, otherwise turn upfield and block toward inside pursuit. The sprint block technique is blocking the defense with your inside shoulder. In order to execute this block, the near back must run parallel to the LOS and attack the widest man on the LOS with an outside approach. The sprint block technique cannot be executed if the widest man runs upfield. If this defensive maneuver occurs, the near back's block is simply to kick out the defensive man with the far back running inside as a lead blocker for the quarterback. (See Diagram 5-10.)

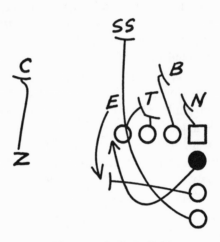

Diagram 5-10: Left 19

The terminology of tailback and fullback has been purposely omitted for the sprint-out play. The reason is that this play can be run from a near or far backfield formation. Because of this multiplicity, the sprint-out could not be described as tailback sprint blocks, or runs upfield, etc. For the tailback may be the lead blocker or the second blocker depending on the backfield formation. Therefore, to simplify learning assignments, the near back and far back are substituted for tailback and fullback when running the quarterback sprint-out. (See Diagram 5-11.)

In executing the sprint-draw though, the tailback and fullback nomenclature is used again, for the sprint-draw can only be run from the base (I formation). The fullback's technique is the same regardless of the defensive front. He must run straight at the onside tackle and block out the first man to show outside of the onside tackle. His man could be a pinching defensive end, blitzing LB'er, looping defensive tackle, corner back or safety blitz, it doesn't matter; the fullback blocks whoever shows outside of onside tackle.

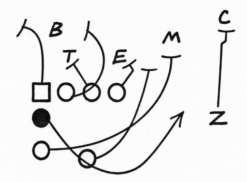

Diagram 5-11: Near-Right 18

Whereas, the fullback is always blocking the same way, the tailback always runs the same technique in receiving the hand-off for the sprint-draw. He must run laterally to the LOS and utilize three steps for the mesh point with the quarterback. These three steps require first a lead step, secondly, a crossover step, thirdly, a plant step and push-off with outside foot. In addition to these three steps, the tailback must keep his

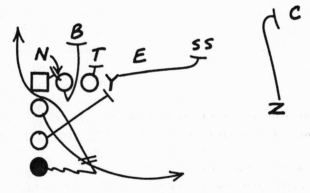

Diagram 5-12: Right 14

body square to the LOS and his eyes on the LOS so that he can "feel" and read the seam. Because the sprint-draw's POA is from end-to-end, the tailback must learn to key certain defensive tendencies. When confronted with an odd defensive front, the tailback should key the nose guard and how he is being blocked. (See Diagram 5-12.)

On an even defense, the tailback changes his key for the onside guard's blocking directions. (See Diagram 5-13.) Undoubtedly, a good tailback will break the sprint-draw repeatedly without keying defensive people because his running instincts take over. But, in teaching the sprint-draw, the tailback should be taught keys to reinforce his total concept of how the sprint-draw develops.

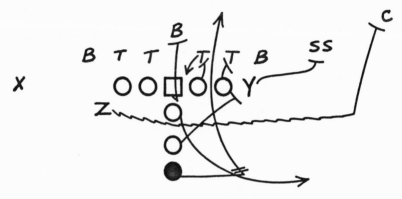

Diagram 5-13: Black-Right 214

PASS BLOCKING RESPONSIBILITIES

Pass blocking responsibilities fall into three categories: 60 blocking, 70 blocking and 80 blocking. In 60 blocking, both backs take one step forward and bend down so that the quarterback can throw quickly without hesitating for fear of hitting a teammate in the helmet. 70 blocking requires the backs to block both sides of the offensive line. Their blocks must be aggressive enough to prevent their being caved in on top of the quarterback and executed so that the defensive people go to the outside. 80 blocking requires the near back to block the number three man aggressively; if three drops, block four man. Far back blocks backside pressure. However, because the quarterback sprint-outs on Green 18-19, both backs are required to sprint-out in tandem the same direction as the quarterback. For offensive line responsibilities this is 80 pass blocking. But the backs must know two different techniques for 80 pass blocking. If 81-82 or 83-84 patterns are called, both backs will split and block opposite sides of the offensive line. The following diagrams will demonstrate 60, 70, and 80 series pass blocking schemes for offensive backs.

In Diagram 5-14, the backs are split to give optimum room for the quarterback. Normally, because of the quick release required in the 60 passing series, the backs will not block anyone. If there is a breakdown in a quarterback-receiver or offensive line blocking, both backs will look for the most inside penetration and block low.

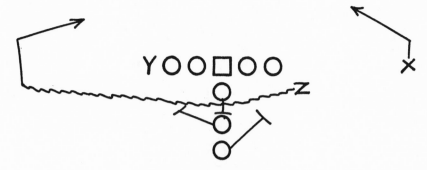

Diagram 5-14: Left 60 Slant

Diagram 5-15 shows both backs blocking the outside perimeter of the blocking cup formed by the offensive linemen. There is no specific man assigned in 70 pass blocking for the backs. As they come up from

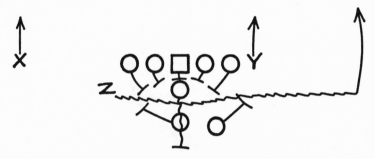

Diagram 5-15: Near-Black Right 271 Go

their stances, they check for stunting LB'ers first. If LB'ers come, backs immediately chop block. With no defensive stunting, both backs sprint to the outside of offensive tackle's area. Just as the offensive linemen are concerned about inside gap, so are the offensive backs. The offensive backs must block the defensive outside pressure to the outside. The rule for knowing which back goes to the right or left is that the fullback always blocks onside when in the I formation. If a near or far backfield alignment is employed, the far back knows automatically he must go to the open backfield side.

In Diagram 5-16, the fullback blocks No. 4 because (Y) stays in on 81-82 patterns and blocks No. 3 man. Of course, if (Y) fails in blocking No. 3, the fullback will help if the No. 4 man drops off. The tailback blocks No. 3. However, if the onside LB'er fires, the running back must be able to block him if the offensive line fails.

In Diagram 5-17, the near back blocks No. 3, not No. 4. The reason

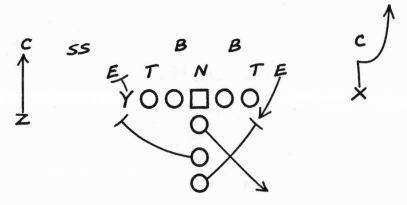

Diagram 5-16: Left 82 Sideline

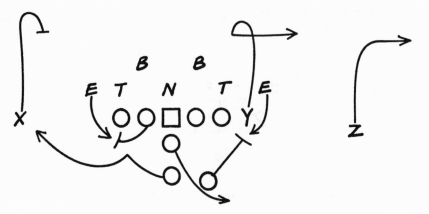

Diagram 5-17: Near-Right 84

being that Y is a receiver not a blocker as in 81-82, and the No. 3 man will not be blocked. The far back blocks No. 3 with help from offside linemen. In fact, if the offside LB'er is not stunting, which frees one of the offside linemen, the far back will check No. 3 and then flare.

SCREEN TECHNIQUE

The screen series in the *Multiple-Motion I Offense* is sequenced off the 80 series or sprint-series look. The back executing the screen is always the tailback when base backfield formation is being used. If far or near formations are used, the back who would be blocking as the far back on the quarterback sprint-out would be the screen man.

The back who is the screen man must know several things. One is that he must appear as if he is going to block the defensive end away from the sprint-out by the quarterback. Normally, both backs block to the same side when the 80 series is employed. Secondly, the screen man must allow the defensive end or outside rush man to run past his outside shoulder. This movement allows the screen man to dip back behind the man he has just blocked. The screen man goes back to an area of about 5-7 yards behind offside tackle. His back will be to the LOS. He must catch the ball standing still. After receiving the ball, he turns to the outside and yells for the screen blockers to move upfield. (See Diagram 5-18.)

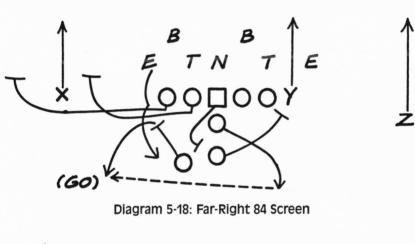

Diagram 5-18: Far-Right 84 Screen

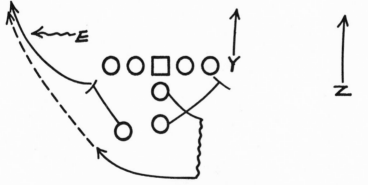

Diagram 5-19: Far-Right 84 Screen

If the defensive end doesn't run, the screen man attacks the flat area and heads toward the sideline. The quarterback, upon seeing no screen man, will run toward the screen man's area and dump a flat pass or abort and throw the ball out-of-bounds in the direction of the screen man. (See Diagram 5-19.) Teams that utilize the 5-2 Defense in which their backside defensive end drops off, present problems for the 80 screen series. Chapter 10 explains how to exploit this defensive maneuver.

6

Utilizing the Pass Receiver
in the Multiple-Motion I

There are many theories on the proper stance for wide receivers. In the *Multiple-Motion I Offense,* the wide receivers are in a 2 pt. stance. The reason is multifold: easier to adjust splits from boundaries, quicker to begin motion, able to see secondary coverage more clearly, able to adjust to LOS, and gives the receiver an upright position so that he can release from the LOS easier. The tight-end (Y) will always be in a 3 pt. stance, for the tight-end is called upon to block tackles as well as he blocks strong-safeties. Therefore, the 3 pt. stance is the only stance that allows this flexibility.

BLOCKING WITH (X) AND (Z)

There are only two kinds of blocks that the *Multiple-Motion I Offense* requires of the split end (X) and flanker (Z). These two blocks are the stalk block and the crackback block.

The stalk block is the most commonly used block for (X) and (Z). The techniques of the stalk block are as follows:

1. Run straight at your assigned man.
2. Break down only when the defensive man reacts to the run instead of the pass.
3. Break down so that you can move laterally as well as you can forward.
4. After breaking down, do not rush out after defensive man, but *stalk* him. Mirror the defensive man's actions.
5. Once the defensive man begins an aggressive move forward, only then should the receiver begin to put a shoulder into the defensive man.
6. As a receiver stalk blocking, allow the defensive man to make an

angle mistake. If the defensive man doesn't move forward, the receiver should remain in a break-down position. Even though the defensive man has not been touched, he is being blocked as long as the receiver remains between the ball carrier and the defensive man to whom he is assigned.

The crackback block is quite opposite of the stalk block. Whereas the stalk block requires finesse and execution can be perfect without physical contact, the crackback block is a block that requires contact and courage with an understanding of crackback rules. The purpose of the crackback is to block inside from a wide receiver position in any of the three defensive areas. (See Diagram 6-1.)

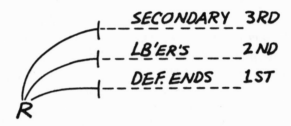

Diagram 6-1: Crackback Blocking

The shoulders of the receiver are parallel to the LOS and he adjusts to the defender's path or to the next defensive area. The *defender applies the force*. The blocking receiver must always stay under control. When in doubt about defensive penetration, the receiver reacts from inside out. Legally, the block must be executed above the waist. If not, the offense can be penalized for 15 yards.

(X) AND (Z) BLOCKING RULES

The blocking rules for the split end (X) and the flanker (Z) can be described in three areas: outside ⅓, middle ⅓, and crackback. In the outside ⅓ and the middle ⅓ the receiver executes the stalk block.

The outside ⅓ simply tells the wide receiver that he must block the outside contain of the defensive secondary. Ideally, the receiver's stalk block should be executed so that the defender will run inside of the receiver's block. The middle ⅓ tells the wide receiver that he should run to the inside of the secondary people playing contain and break down so that he can block the defense to the outside such as a kickout block on a defensive end by a blocking fullback. (See Diagrams 6-2 and 6-3.)

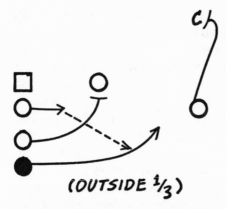

(OUTSIDE ⅓)

Diagram 6-2: Outside ⅓ Blocking

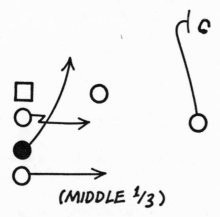

(MIDDLE ⅓)

Diagram 6-3: Middle ⅓ Blocking

As a general rule, the wide receiver blocks middle ⅓ whenever the ball is being run inside the offensive tackle. If the ball is being run outside of the tackle, the wide receiver's rule is either outside ⅓ or crackback. Examples of the ball going to the outside in which the wide receiver blocks outside ⅓ on one play and crackbacks on another are the quarterback sprint-out and the toss play respectively.

In the quarterback sprint-out (18-19), the quarterback attempts to give a false key to lure the LB'ers into thinking that the ball will be passed. If the wide receiver cracked down on the LB'er, the quarterback's sprint-out run would be diagnosed quickly. The secondary would be flying up for the run and very little success would occur from the sequencing of the sprint series. Whereas, if the wide receiver "ran off his man," then stalk blocked his defensive man to the outside ⅓, the quarterback would have a better running lane to operate in.

The 26-27 Toss is such an easy read or key for the onside LB'er that he would stop the play immediately unless he is blocked.The wide receiver has a great angle to block the onside LB'er, therefore, the crackback rule applies. The wide receivers do not need to count people to see if they are blocking the #4 man or the #3 man. The main concern for the wide receiver is to check his three defensive areas as shown in Diagram 6-1. Moreover, the wide receiver must keep in mind the rule regulating the legality of crackback blocks.

The blocking rules for (X) and (Z) can change dramatically in a multiple attack if their blocking assignments are not clarified. In the *Multiple-Motion I Offense,* there are many formations that could make it impossible for (X) and (Z) to remember their assignments if they did not understand the philosophy of middle ⅓, outside ⅓, and crackback. The *Multiple-Motion I Offense* reduces the wide receiver's blocking assignments to simplistic terms—various formations appear complicated, but execute simply.

(Y) BLOCKING

The tight-end (Y) has more varied blocking assignments than any other offensive player in the *Multiple-Motion I Offense.* The tight-end must be able to execute six blocks: drive block, double-team, reach, stalk block, fold, and combo block. Undoubtedly, the tight-end position in football has undergone more changes than any other position in football. The *Multiple-Motion I Offense's* tight-end's responsibilities certainly reflect the modern trend of this changing position which requires so much versatility.

The following blocking rules apply for (Y) in the *Multiple-Motion I Offense:*

Sprint Draw (14-15)— —Block force; 6-2 defense block LB'er. When blocking force the tight-end must release outside (so as to gain width on POA) and stalk block the force.

Quarterback Sprint-out (18-19) —Block #3 man if on or inside (4-4 defense would be an example). Otherwise, double-team the #2 man. If #2 man disappears inside of offensive tackle, (Y) continues inside and blocks onside LB'er. If offensive tackle and (Y) have a double-team whereas the #2 man is being controlled by the offensive tackle, (Y) should bump off (combo block) and pick up onside LB'er.

22-23 Lead	—Block widest man.
24-25 Lead	—Block 3 on or inside; otherwise double-team 2.
26-27 Toss	—Reach rule (Chapter 2).
28-29 Option	—Block 3 on or inside; otherwise double-team 2.
30-31 Trap	—Slam widest man, release and block middle ⅓.
32-33 Veer	—Block 3 on or inside; otherwise release and block force.
34-35 Veer	—Block 3 on or inside; otherwise double-team 2.
38-39 Veer	—Block 3 on or inside; otherwise block force.
40-41 Counter	—Block 3; vs. 6-2 defense. The tight-end must fold block between guard-tackle in order to block the onside LB'er who is 3. If the LB'er is shading to the outside of the defensive tackle, still treat him as the #3 man because the offensive blocking philosophy in the *Multiple-Motion I Offense* is the defense as the offensive line recognizes it.

The flanker (Z) in the *Multiple-Motion I Offense* is usually split as a wide receiver. However, the flanker is employed as a tight-end in the black formation. The black formation thrusts new blocking assignments upon (Z) when the ball is run to his formation side. Therefore, (Z) must be able to adapt from his wide receiver role to that of a tight-end's. If a team is blessed with two individuals who are flankers, one could be used as (Z) when black formation is being employed and the other for wide receiver so that mental assignments could be minimized.

Furthermore, if one flanker is more useful as a blocker than the other flanker, the blocking flanker could be employed for formations that require (Z) to block as a tight-end. In addition to using two different types of athletes for the flanker position, the tight-end position could be used to alleviate the blocking responsibilities of (Z). If there are two (Y's) that can play the position well, use one of the (Y's) as a flanker when utilizing black formation or formations that require a flanker to block as a tight-end. This strategy requires no extra learning since (Z) blocks (Y's) rules when in the black formation.

The tight-end, flanker, and the split-end are taught fundamental pass receiving rules that are instrumental in successful passing attacks. These rules are:

PASS RECEIVING RULES

1. Take the same stance that you take on running plays. Don't telegraph the pass.
2. Always expect the defense to try to hold you in. "I didn't get out" is not an acceptable excuse. By ready to use head fakes and release techniques, for YOU MUST GET OUT.
3. Always run your patterns at full, controlled speed. We cannot get the correct timing at half speed.
4. Keep your eyes on the ball. Your first responsibility is to CATCH THE BALL. After you make the catch think about additional yardage and scoring. CONCENTRATE on the ball—this is the most important single factor in pass receiving.
5. When we are on offense and the ball is thrown, it is not a "Free" ball, it is ours, GO GET IT. Never allow interceptions.
6. Run angles and not curves, for the receiver running sharp angles is much more difficult to cover.
7. Pass receivers are made...not born. They are made by practice, day after day, until all of your moves and receiving become second nature. Whenever possible, have a football in your hands. Play catch with your partner. Never let the ball become a stranger to you.
8. Talk to QB when you have a chance. NOT IN THE HUDDLE. Tell your coaches what you can do—your best bet for 3rd down passes, 3rd and 7-10 yards, your best long pattern.
9. Learn the tendencies of the defensive backs: if they gamble, guess with you, play tight or loose, inside or out, their speed. Have a book on all of your opponents.

10. As you approach the ball, keep your stride even and smooth. If your stride is broken and uneven, the ball appears to jump in mid-air.

11. The sidelines and end zone lines are your enemies. Always know your relative position to them. Respect them, do not let them bother you in catching the ball—the catch comes first. The officials will never call you "in bounds" if you drop the ball.

12. On a long pass keep your hands and arms in running position until the instant before the ball gets there. To bring your hands up too soon will break your stride, reduce your speed and destroy your balance.

13. On the long passes cradle the ball and keep the little fingers overlapping, so the ball will not go through your fingers. On short passes, catch it much the same way you would catch a hard-hit ball.

14. Get in the habit of going all out after the ball every time—regardless of how it is thrown. Soon the great catches will become routine.

15. Level off for the goal post as quickly as possible, for one missed tackle could mean a touchdown.

16. Fake the man—not the area.

17. In practice, run hard three steps after every catch. In other words, simulate game conditions.

18. Our receivers are football players—not just pass receivers. *We will block.*

19. Know your pass offense and carry out all patterns as if the ball is being thrown to you.

20. If necessary to jump for a ball when men are covering you—watch the ball and be sure your timing is right. FIGHT FOR THE BALL.

21. Practice catching bad passes as you are expected to catch any ball near you. Anyone can catch the perfect pass.

22. You must learn to turn or snap the head around quickly as you make the final break on a pass pattern, so you can locate the ball as quickly as possible.

23. Hustle up to the line from the huddle. Be alert—get off the ground; alert football players do not stay on the ground.

24. With a kick or bop pass pattern that is to the outside (corner) then receiver should fake inside and release to the outside. And vice versa.

25. Must be able to get open in a one-on-one situation.

26. Must have a terrific desire to catch the ball.
27. Great receivers make the big play.

TECHNIQUES OF CATCHING THE BALL

A good receiver will catch the ball with "liquid" hands. Liquid means to give with the ball, for it has a built-in set of springs and will jump out if you fight it. Relax completely as the balls comes toward you. Follow the ball with the eyes all the way into the hands. As the ball is approaching you, eliminate all thought from the mind except catching the football. A great receiver's concentration should be so great that there is an unawareness of defenders being present.

Position of the hands is vital to success. A ball thrown directly at chest level or higher should be caught with the thumbs in. If the ball is thrown below the chest level, the thumbs should be turned out. Always try to get the body in front of the ball on short passes. A ball thrown on the outside and away from the receiver should be caught with the thumbs out. On long passes, never allow the inside arm to be in a position to blind you from seeing the ball. A cardinal rule to remember on every pass is that if the receiver cannot possibly catch the football, he should not permit the opponent to catch it.

PASSING TREE

In Diagram 6-4, the passing tree of (Y), (Z), and (X) are detailed. The patterns shown are standard routes used by most teams. These routes will be coordinated in the *Multiple-Motion I Offense* in later chapters. The reader should only familiarize himself with the routes as they are described.

DIAGONAL:	A medium (5-10 yds.) crossing pattern by (Y) to take advantage of LB'ers who pass-drop quickly.
DELAY:	A medium pass in which the beginning of the route shows blocking for a two-count.
FLAT:	A quick 5 yd. pass to the receiver as he turns to his outside immediately after leaving the LOS.
HOOK:	10-12 yd. pass in which the receiver pivots to his inside.

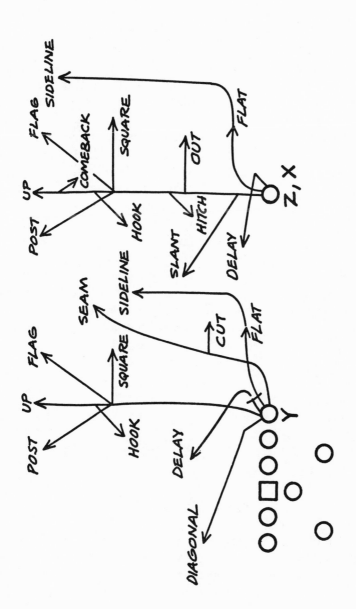

Diagram 6-4: Passing Tree of Y, X, Z

SQUARE:	10-12 yd. route with a 90° pivot to the outside.
SEAM:	For (Y), this is a pattern where he releases outside defensive end pressure and runs in a seam between defensive back pressure. Ball will be thrown to outside shoulder. For (X) and (Z) this is two routes in one. If they can beat middle ⅓ coverage on a go pattern, they continue up the field. If the defensive backfield is playing too deep, the seam turns into a 10-12 yd. hook.
SIDELINE:	The route begins with a flat route and then turns up the sideline looking for a pass inside.
POST:	15-20 yd. route in which the receiver pivots on a 45° angle to the inside.
UP:	Straight pattern up the field.
FLAG:	15-20 yd. route in which the receiver pivots on a 45° angle to the outside.
GO:	A deep pattern in which the receiver runs at the defender's inside shoulder and breaks downfield off the outside shoulder of the defender.
COMEBACK:	15-20 yd. route in which the receiver pivots sharply to sideline and curls in.
SLANT:	A quick 45° angle route from the LOS.
OUT:	A 5 yard square route.
HITCH:	A 5 yard hook pattern.

COMBINATION ROUTES

Combination Routes are used only in the sprint series of the *Multiple-Motion I Offense*—Green 18-19. The name of the combination route describes the maneuver for the inside man only. (Y) and (X) will always have inside and outside routes respectively to remember, whereas (Z) has to learn both routes on all combination routes. The reason being that (Z) can be employed as a slot man or wide receiver in a pro set. These combination routes are memorized by the receivers. Each combination route is designed to take advantage of a defensive weakness. Subsequent chapters illustrate how this is done. (See Diagrams 6-5 through 6-14.)

CROSSING PATTERN RULE

The crossing pattern rule is to be applied for the receiver who is not the primary receiver or in the primary combination route. The rule simply means that the receiver will run a post pattern unless he reads the free safety playing deep. If the safety is deep, the receiver breaks off the post pattern and runs underneath the safety.

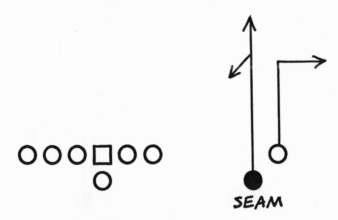

Diagram 6-5: Seam Combination

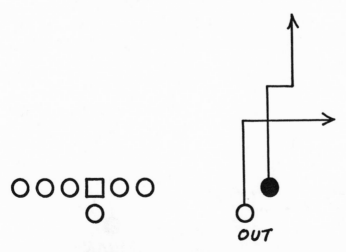

Diagram 6-6: Out Combination

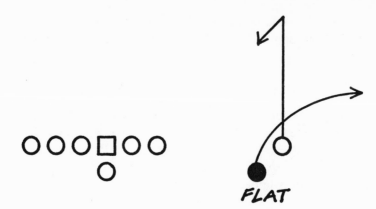

FLAT

Diagram 6-7: Flat Combination

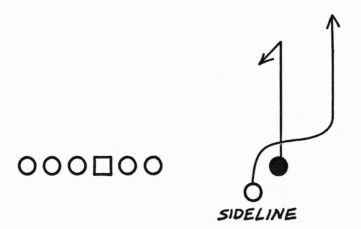

SIDELINE

Diagram 6-8: Sideline Combination

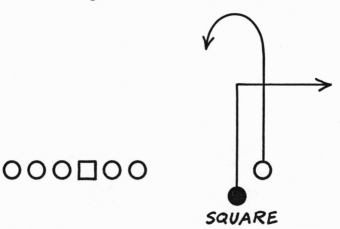

SQUARE

Diagram 6-9: Square Combination

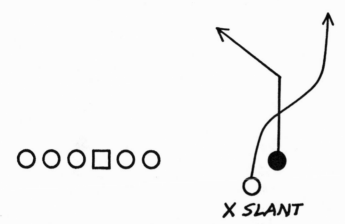

Diagram 6-10: Slant Combination

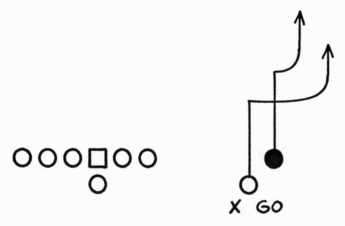

Diagram 6-11: Go Combination

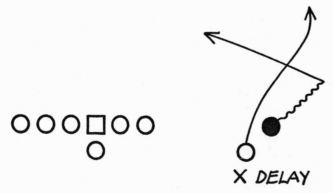

Diagram 6-12: Delay Combination

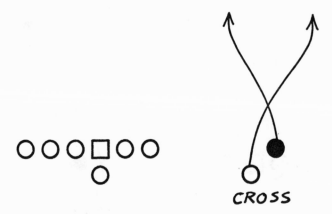

CROSS

Diagram 6-13: Cross Combination

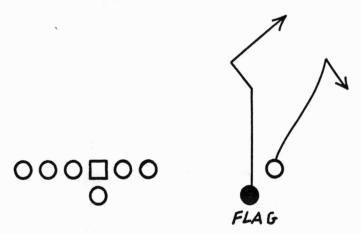

FLAG

Diagram 6-14: Flag Combination

In Diagram 6-15, (Y) is not involved in the Go combination route. Because (Y) is not involved, he runs a crossing pattern. The free safety is playing deep, so (Y) breaks off this post and runs underneath the free safety's coverage parallel to the LOS.

In Diagram 6-16, X is not involved in the seam combination. Therefore, X runs the crossing pattern and breaks for a post pattern because the free safety has come up on the middle ⅓ coverage.

60 SERIES PATTERNS

The 60 Series in the *Multiple-Motion I Offense* is designed for quick routes and passes. There are three primary routes that (X) and (Z)

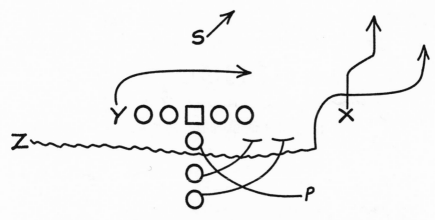

Diagram 6-15: Left-Green 218 Go

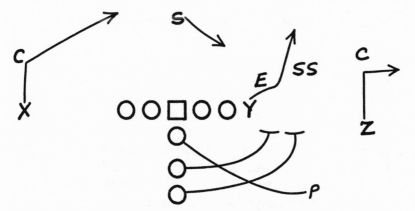

Diagram 6-16: Right-Green 18 Seam

run in the 60 Series ((Y) blocks on all 60 plays). These routes are out, slant, and Hitch. ((Z) runs automatic motion for the 60 Series.) The out and slant require three steps by the receivers before breaking on their patterns. The hitch pattern requires five steps. Diagrams 6-17, 6-18, and 6-19 show the three 60 Series patterns.

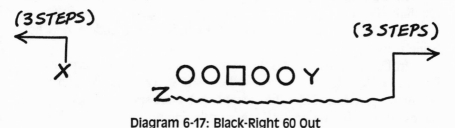

Diagram 6-17: Black-Right 60 Out

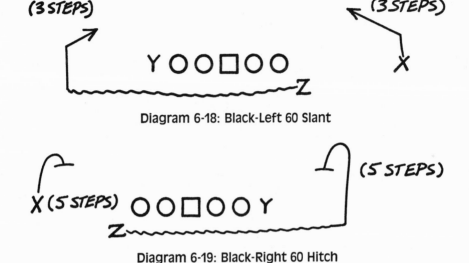

Diagram 6-18: Black-Left 60 Slant

Diagram 6-19: Black-Right 60 Hitch

70 SERIES PATTERNS

The 70 Series is the drop-back passing series with all three receivers being utilized. Each receiver is given a designated number which indicates if he is the primary receiver. If he is not the primary receiver, he will run the same route every time a 70 Series play is called. (Z) is 1, (Y) is 2, and (X) is 3. (Z's) automatic route is post or comeback. The reason (Z) has an option is that if the middle ⅓ of the secondary is going to be utilized with another receiver, he will run a comeback instead of post. (Y's) automatic route is a hook. (X's) automatic route is an up pattern. The following diagrams will illustrate 70 Series plays.

In Diagram 6-20, (Z) is the primary receiver because one was the last digit. Since the pattern called was a hook, (Z) runs his hook pattern. (Y) runs his automatic route (hook) because he was not the primary receiver. (X) also runs his automatic route (up), because (Z) was the primary receiver.

In Diagram 6-21, (Y) is the primary receiver because two was the last digit. Therefore (Y) runs the pattern called diagonal. (X) and (Z) run their automatic patterns. (Z) runs a post because the middle ⅓ is not being used.

In Diagram 6-22, (X) is the primary receiver because three was the last digit. (X) runs the pattern called a post. (Z) and (Y) run their automatic patterns. This time though (Z) exercises his option of two routes given in his automatic 70 series rule. He runs a comeback instead of a post because (X) is using the middle ⅓ on his post pattern. If (Z) ran

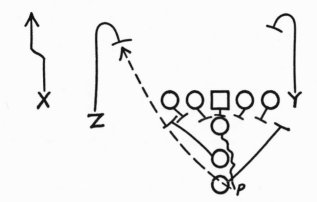

Diagram 6-20: Twins-Right 71 Hook

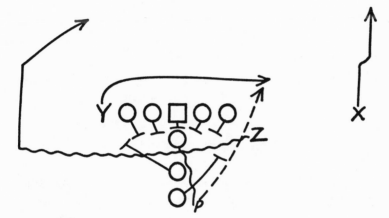

Diagram 6-21: Black-Left 172 Diagonal

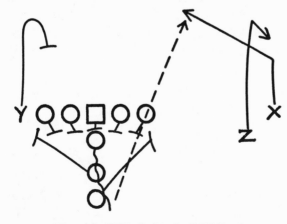

Diagram 6-22: Twins-Left 73 Post

his post, there could be a collision. Moreover, the secondary coverage could cover two receivers with one defensive man.

The 70 series utilizes the "hot receiver" rule that so many passing teams employ. Hot receiver refers to a receiver who will be passed to automatically if there is a blitz. In the 70 series, the tight-end (Y) is the hot receiver. As (Y) releases from the LOS, his attention must be focused on the onside LB'er. This focus allows (Y) to know if he will be passed to immediately or not. If the onside LBer vacates, (Y) receives a quick pass. (See Diagram 6-23.)

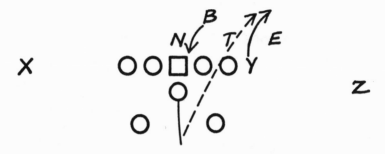

Diagram 6-23: Y as "Hot Receiver"

80 SERIES PATTERNS

The 80 series is an extension of the sprint series passing game. The quarterback sets up differently and there are no combination routes. Yet the 80 series mirrors the sprint series in backfield action. There are three plays off the 80 series not counting the screen series. These plays are 81-82, 83-84, and 83-84 flood. 81-82 are individual routes with the primary receiver being the receiver on the side of the play called. The secondary receiver runs a crossing pattern. (Y) blocks only on 81-82. (See Diagram 6-24 and 6-25.)

Diagram 6-24: Right 82 Sideline

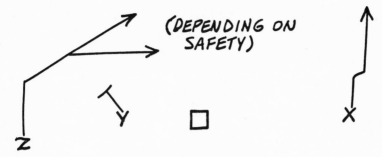

Diagram 6-25: Left 82 Go

The 83-84 pass pays are set patterns. (Y) does a hook, (X) a post, and (Z) an out. (See Diagram 6-26.) (Y's) hook is to the inside and then slide to the outside. The reason being is to take advantage of the strong-safety's dilemma.

The 83-84 flood passes are set patterns also. All three receivers run hook patterns with the near back running a flat route off (Y's) rear end. (See Diagram 6-27.)

(Y's) route in the 83-84 flood is opposite of the 83-84 pass play. In the flood pattern, (Y) slides inside so as to allow (Z) to hook. The running back's route to the flat is to put extra pressure on the strong-safety. Cover (Z) or running back?

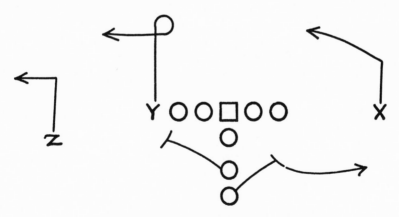

Diagram 6-26: Left 83

The screen series is sequenced off 80 series action. Therefore, (Y), (X), and (Z) run designed patterns for false keys. These patterns will always be *up* patterns. Once the defense recognizes the screen, the three receivers must be under enough control so that they can break down and stalk block effectively. Chapter 10 describes in detail how the *Multiple-Motion I Offense* utilizes the 60, 70, 80 and screen series effectively against various defenses.

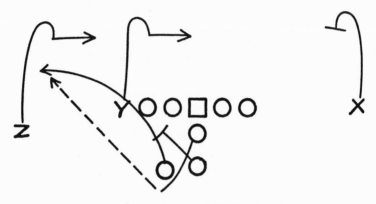

Diagram 6-27: Near-Left 83 Flood

7

Developing the Sprint Series

The *Multiple-Motion I Offense* utilizes the I-formation as its basic set. The plays following will be sequenced according to play numbers, not as sets or formations.

DEVELOPING THE SPRINT-DRAW

The sprint-draw, one of the most exciting plays in football, that can easily be seen as it develops for the fan in the stands. The defense, however, can become totally confused in attempting to stop it. Moreover, with the use of motion and the creation of different sets, the sprint-draw can appear to the defense as several plays.

There are several variations of the sprint-draw. Many coaches utilize completely different techniques than the sprint-draw technique illustrated here. We feel our sprint-draw (14-15) is the best for high school and college players because it doesn't demand outstanding speed on the part of the tailback, but the ability to run with his eyes open. Sprint-draw and the use of multiple-motion is as follows:

ON TACKLE:	Block 2.
ON GUARD:	Block 1.
CENTER:	Block 0; Off-Side.
OFF-SIDE GUARD:	Block 1 Over or Outside; otherwise 2 ("If").
OFF-SIDE TACKLE:	Block 2 Over or Outside; otherwise 3 ("If").
Y:	Block Outside Release, Block Force; vs. 6-2 Block LB'er.
X:	Block Middle ⅓.
Z:	Block Middle ⅓.
FB:	Block out 1st man to show outside Offensive Tackle.

RB: Block 3 steps to sideline, 90° plant step; run to daylight.

QUARTERBACK ACTION   Sprint action, hand-off with 2 hands as
& ALERTS: deep as possible—don't take too flat an angle. Carry out pass fake.

The rules above are consistent throughout the development of the sprint-draw or Play 14-15. As shown in Diagrams 7-1, 7-2, 7-3, and 7-4, the sprint-draw can be run effectively from different sets. Moreover, with the use of motion in Diagram 7-3, we have shown the same look as Diagram 7-2. Conversely, if we had called Diagram 7-2 Twins-Left 114, it would have mirrored Diagram 7-3. (See Diagram 7-5.)

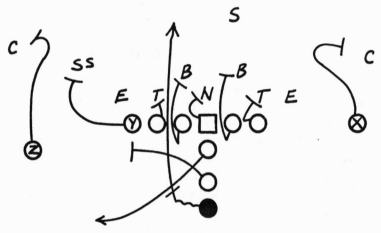

Diagram 7-1: Sprint-Draw (Left 15) 5-2 Defense

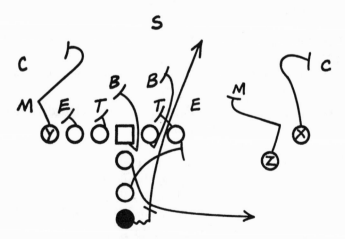

Diagram 7-2: Sprint-Draw Right (Twins-Left 14) 4-4 Defense

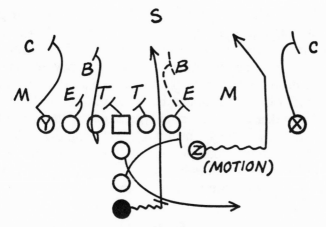

Diagram 7-3: Sprint-Draw Right (Black-Left 214) 6-2 Defense

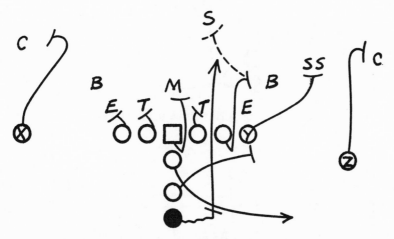

Diagram 7-4: Sprint-Draw Right (Right 14) 4-3 Defense

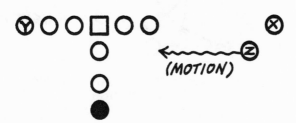

Diagram 7-5

Sprint-draw is not a play to be used just on third down or passing situations. It is an offensive weapon that should be used 15-20 times a game. The sprint-draw has its limitations like any other offensive play. 6-2 defense presents more problems for the sprint-draw than any other defense. The main reason for the 6-2 being such a problem is that the onside 6-2 linebacker is difficult to block. A variation of blocking the onside 6-2 linebacker could be a slam type action by the onside tackle. The tackle would slam the #2 man while eyeballing the LB'er all the time and release inside or outside to block the LB, depending on his flow. (See Diagram 7-6.) But, as in any football play, 6-2 linebacker can be victimized by the sprint-draw pass (Green 14-15). (See Diagram 7-7.)

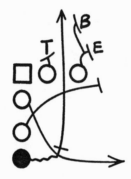

Diagram 7-6: Sprint-Draw vs. 6-2 LB'er

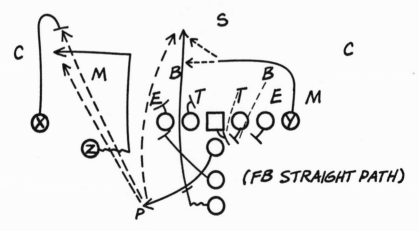

Diagram 7-7: Sprint-Draw Pass (Twins-Right
Green 215) 6-2 Defense

DEVELOPING THE SPRINT-DRAW PASS

ON TACKLE:	Block 2.
ON GUARD:	Block 1.
CENTER:	Block 0; Off-Side.
OFF-SIDE GUARD:	Block 1 Over or Outside; otherwise 2 ("If").
OFF-SIDE TACKLE:	Block 2 Over or Outside; otherwise 3 ("If").
Y:	Flat pattern; (unless away, crossing pattern).
X:	Crossing pattern (unless onside, then hook pattern, slide if ball is late).
Z:	Hook pattern unless twins or black is used, then assume Y's responsibility (flat pattern).
FB:	Block widest man with head outside. (Sprint block as mentioned earlier).
RB:	Slice technique, fake and block off-tackle area.
QUARTERBACK ACTION & ALERTS:	Sprint action, fake draw to R as deep as possible, find out how end is being blocked. Check flat first.

Motion is not necessary in Diagram 7-7 if you isolate the play. (Chapter 1 details rules for motion.) But if you tie motion in with a sweep series, drop-back series, sprint-draw series, etc., as will be shown later, the motion becomes invaluable in gaining blocking strength and probing defensive weaknesses. Diagram 7-7 shows sprint-draw play-action from twins.

Generally, this play is more effective to the tight-end (Y) side. The reason being that the sprint-out run by the QB can be set up better if play-action can be shown on (Y's) side. Undoubtedly, the strength of any offense must be that it can sequence so as to gain advantage against the defensive keys. If linebackers are crowding the LOS and ignoring the sprint-out action of the QB, the sprint-out pass must be used. Conversely, if LB'ers are playing off the LOS and are flying to their pass responsibilities when shown sprint-out action by QB, sprint-draw must be used.

Diagram 7-8 is a good example of probing defensive weakness with the use of motion. If the contain man, LB'er, or safety do not pick up (Z) in his motion away from the play, sprint-pass combinations are going to be covered by one defensive back. Moreover, if LB'er does pick up (Z), sprint-draw will have no LB'er to block. If monster covers motion, we can adjust the fullback's path so he can lead through the sprint-draw. (See Diagram 7-8.) The list of possibilities can go on with the unlimited use of motion. The important idea though is that the probing of defensive weaknesses is futile if the offense is not sequenced.

Another example of using motion to probe defensive weaknesses is shown in Diagram 7-9.

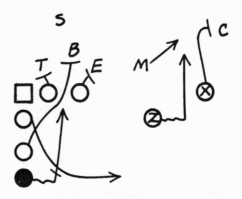

Diagram 7-8

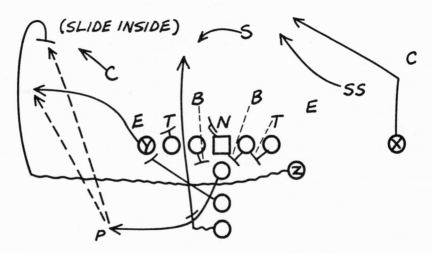

Diagram 7-9: Sprint-Draw Pass (Black-Left Green 115) 5-2 Defense

If (Z), as he goes in motion, is adjusted by the defense with secondary (4 deep) rotation, the tight end (Y) should be open on his flat pattern. The reason being that the safety will have very little time in getting to his proper position in the flat. Naturally, if the strong-safety (SS) covers man, it will give our QB the ability to check off to a weakside pass with our tailback in the flat. This creates LB coverage on a tailback. (See Diagram 7-10.)

If the contain men in a defense are playing a soft technique and floating to onside passing zones, thereby relieving the LB'ers of any outside responsibilities, the sprint-draw series must employ the sprint-out run by the QB.

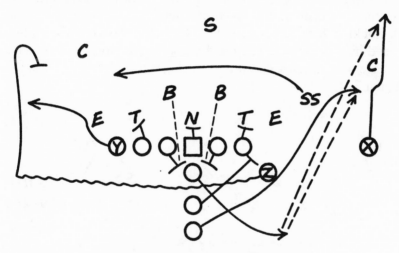

Diagram 7-10: Tailback Pass to Flat

DEVELOPING THE SPRINT-OUT

ON TACKLE:	Block 2.
ON GUARD:	Block 1.
CENTER:	Block 0; Off-Side.
OFF-SIDE GUARD:	Block 1 Over or Outside; otherwise 2 ("If").
OFF-SIDE TACKLE:	Block 2 Over or Outside; otherwise 3 ("If").
Y:	3 on or inside; otherwise double team 2.
X:	Middle ⅓.
Z:	Outside ⅓.

NEAR BACK:	Widest man on LOS with Sprint-Block technique.
FAR BACK:	Sprint to 1 yd. beyond near Back's block, help if help is needed, if not, block next man to show.
QUARTERBACK ACTION & ALERTS:	Sprint action to point, read near back's block, react accordingly. (Raise arm as if passing).

As mentioned in Diagram 7-7, the sprint-draw pass is more effective to (Y's) side when the sprint-out is employed. The reason being that (Y) must go outside of the defensive end (5-2 Def.) to run his route on the sprint-draw pass. As you continue to run the sprint-draw pass in a game, the end begins to play his position softer or he takes a poor pursuit angle thinking that (Y) is going outside again as he does on the sprint-out pass and his worries of getting caught inside wane. Sprint-out run takes advantage of a defensive end who is playing soft or crashing inside. (See Diagram 7-11.)

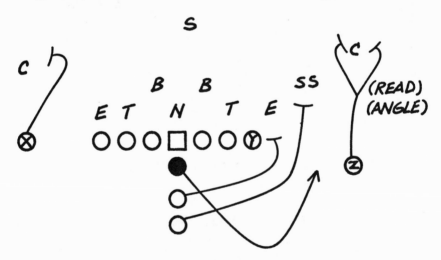

Diagram 7-11: Sprint-Out Run (Right 18) 5-2 Defense

EXAMPLES OF MULTIPLE-MOTION I
ON SPRINT-OUT RUN

Again, as I continue to emphasize, sequencing is so vital to offensive productivity. Diagrams 7-12 and 7-13 are good examples for illustrating motion to your advantage and the sequencing of one more play to the sprint series—the sprint-out pass.

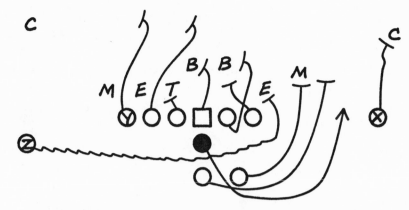

Diagram 7-12: Sprint-Out (Far Left 218) 4-4 Defense

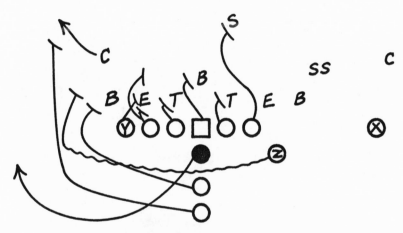

Diagram 7-13: Sprint-Out (Black-Left 119) 6-1 Defense

DEVELOPING THE SPRINT-OUT PASS

Sprint-out pass can be utilized into several combination routes (Chapter 6). For our illustration we will take the *out* combination pattern. (See Diagrams 7-14 and 7-15.)

ON TACKLE:	Block 2.
ON GUARD:	Block 1.
CENTER:	Block 0; Off-Side.
OFF-SIDE GUARD:	Block 1 Over or Outside; otherwise 2 ("If").
OFF-SIDE TACKLE:	Block 2 Over or Outside; otherwise 3 ("If").

Y, X, Z: Combination patterns (Chapter 6).
NEAR BACK: 3, if 3 drops, block 4 with sprint block
                                technique.
FAR BACK: Sprint to 1 yd. beyond near back's

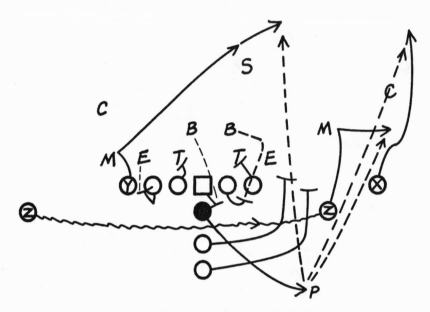

Diagram 7-14: Sprint-Out Pass (Left Green 218 Out) 4-4 Defense

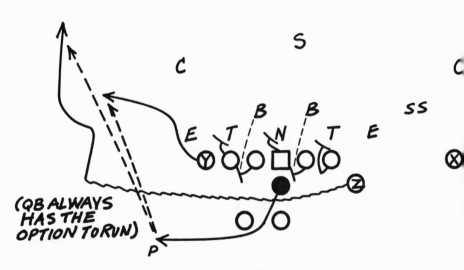

Diagram 7-15: Sprint-Out Pass (Near-Black Left Green 119 Out) 5-2 Defense

block, block contain if help needed, if not, block next man to show.

QUARTERBACK ACTION & ALERTS: Sprint action; read pattern—have to be aware of the defensive end's play.

The following examples will depict the use of motion in demonstrating how one play (sprint-out pass) can be disguised into looking like several plays. (See Diagram 7-16.)

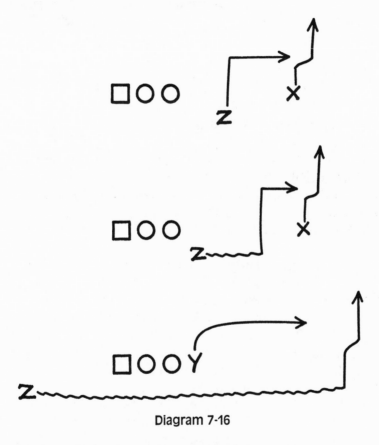

Diagram 7-16

Motion will do several things to the defense:

1. Possibly force the safety to play strong-safety position.
2. Possibly make the defense play man-to-man secondary.
3. Possibly catch the defensive secondary so there is no 2-man coverage at all.
4. Possibly make the onside end (who thought he was the away end from power) play soft thinking that there is no coverage to back up pass plays to his side.

The above list can go on. But the four possibilities we look at from our press box are these. If the safety is forced to play strong-safety, we will begin to throw deep to the now converted safety with the crossing-post pattern. Furthermore, if the safety who is the converted strong-safety remains deep in the rotation, the QB will run the ball with a distinct advantage, for there will be no force to stop the QB if he decides to run on his sprint-out pass which he always has the option to do. If man coverage in the secondary occurs, we at least know their coverage and can pass away from our motion with flood patterns to our backs. (The most difficult pass responsibility in football is to cover a back with a linebacker, especially high school.)

In addition, we can also call many crossing patterns which are difficult to defend against in a man-to-man secondary play. If motion creates a breakdown, offensively we should have an excellent play if we execute. Surprisingly enough, if motion is used not as a decoy, but is blended into the offense with purpose, poor defensive secondary coverage will occur more than many coaches think possible. All coaches dream of the possibility of passing to two receivers with one-man coverage. If the defensive end plays soft, the offense can adjust with the QB sprint-out, sprint-out pass or come off tackle with basic power plays (Chapter 8).

Other examples of the *Multiple-Motion I Offense* in the sprint series are as follows:

If corner rotates slowly to motion, (Z) back should be open on square-out. (See Diagram 7-17.) Corner rotates quickly, to outside, tight-end (Y) will be open in seam. (Y) must catch ball to his outside shoulder and split the seam between safety and corner. If strong-safety covers man-to-man, QB should yell "GO" on his sprint-out and run for daylight, for only the safety will be the *force*. (Y) will be taking the cornerback to his seam pattern. (Z) will stalk-block strong-safety with additional help from running back.

In Diagram 7-18 the advantage is the crackback angle for (Z) on the defensive end. On-side offensive tackle has a relatively easy seal block on onside linebacker. Cornerback must be stalk blocked by (X) (split-end). Remember there is tremendous pressure placed on the CB's—maintain outside leverage for runs and play pass defense (in this defensive set he would most likely have deep-outside ⅓, which would create even more pressure). Is the QB sprinting out to pass or run? With this uncertainty, the cornerback will usually play pass first allowing "time to be bought" for the split-end stalk blocking him, thus allowing the QB to gain valuable yardage.

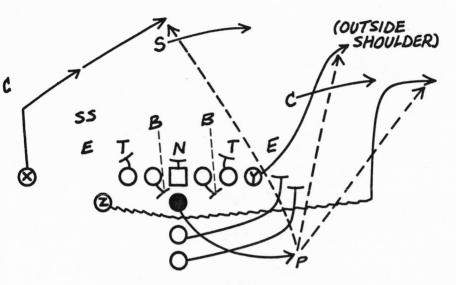

Diagram 7-17: Sprint-Out Pass (Black-Right Green 218 Seam) 5-2 Defense

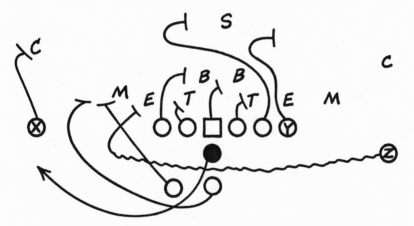

Diagram 7-18: Sprint-Out Run (Far-Right 119) 4-4 Defense

If the slot formation has been used for a run or pass play, regardless of its effectiveness, the defense must adjust to its strength. Thereby, the sprint-draw away from the slot can leave (Y) (tight-end) trying to find a force. (See Diagram 7-19.) If the strong-safety rotates to middle ⅓ when motion goes away, the safety must now change his defensive posture quickly and correctly. Moreover, if cornerback is slow in sliding to the outside, the sprint-draw could bounce to the outside with no contain to

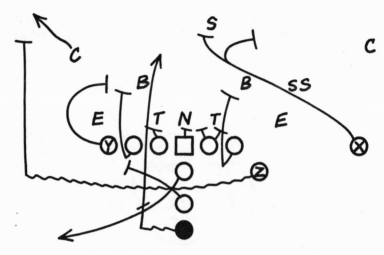

Diagram 7-19: Sprint-Draw (Black-Left 115)
5-2 Defense (Eagle)

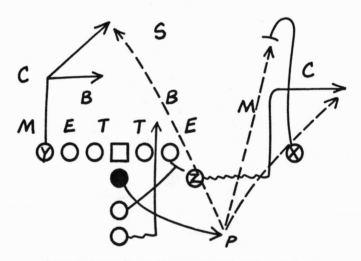

Diagram 7-20: Sprint-Draw Pass (Black-Left
Green 214) 6-2 Defense

stop a long gainer. Sprint-draw pass away from the slot can be even more effective with the defensive secondary scrambling to pass responsibilities.

Sprint-draw pass vs. 6-2 defense can take advantage of two defensive weaknesses. (See Diagram 7-20.) On the flat pattern run by (Z), it takes a very fast outside LB'er to stop this quick pass play to (Z). Moreover, onside LB'er must respond to sprint-draw action and thus restrict his hook zone area. This play action enables (X) (split-end) to slide in the "free" zone area. (Y) (tight-end) does his normal crossing pattern (when pass play is away) and reacts accordingly to safety's defensive posture.

If the defense is playing the slot straight, sprint-out will most likely be unsuccessful. Yet, this play can be excellent if the defense has been rotating or slanting to offensive strength. (See Diagram 7-21.) If defensive end has been crashing hard when strength is away, the play should have good results. Again, play selection should be based on defensive weaknesses, not on hope or guesswork.

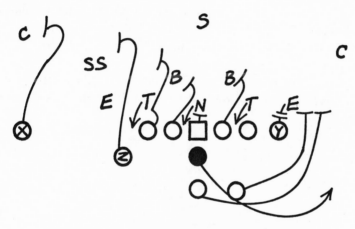

Diagram 7-21: Sprint-Out (Near Black Right 18)
5-2 Angle Defense

TECHNIQUES OF THE SPRINT SERIES

Sprint-out series must be coached with specific techniques. Line blocking, sprint-block of the backs, QB technique, receivers' responsibilities, etc., are described in earlier chapters.

The consistency which you strive for in offense must be detailed in the sprint series. *Everyone* must have a total picture in his mind on how the sprint series develops. I am not encouraging an offensive tackle to learn the QB's position. However, an offensive tackle must know that when he blocks offside on the sprint-draw (14-15), he must bide as much time as possible when blocking a 5-2 def. tackle with the hinge block technique. Granted, it is an easy block if the def. tackle pursues an outside angle. The sprint-draw, however, is a slow-developing play, and more than once an offside def. tackle has made the tackle on the tailback when the offside tackle thought the play was already past him. These are small coaching points, but an offense will lack consistency without constant mentioning of them.

Listed are more of these "small" details in the sprint-series:

Center

The center has an easy block on a 5-2 nose man when running the sprint-draw (14-15). He does not fire-out, but waits (not on heels) for the nose guard to angle one way or another. The center's block is then right or left down the LOS depending on nose guard's path. *We are not interested in depth, but width.* 4-4 defense the center has to show pass for a two count, then chase offside LB'er. The block must be a stalk-block technique (stay on your feet). There is an adjustment that the center has to be prepared for if the offside tackle is crashing hard. (See Diagram 7-22.)

The center sometimes has to fold-block the offside linebacker in order to escape the traffic of your offside guard blocking the 4-4 tackle on an inside slant.

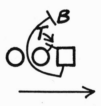

Diagram 7-22: Sprint-Draw (Right 14) 4-4 Defense (offside defensive tackle pinching in)

Guards

Guard play in the sprint-draw (14-15) is consistent in technique. Except for the 6-2 defense, both guards must show pass (count to two) and stack block the number one man in 5-2 defense, normally linebackers. (See Diagram 7-23.)

The guards must always strive to remain clear of any traffic along the LOS and pursue their LB'ers with balance and control. Stay on your

Diagram 7-23: Guard Blocking in Sprint-Draw

feet and screen block or stalk block your man. Remember, the play has more chances of success if time elapses in your warding the defensive man. In the 4-4 defense, the onside guard must fold block and offside guard use his "if" rule (Chapter 2). The 6-2 defense offside guard must fold to the inside to get "if" rule (offside LB'er). Onside guard blocks number one as always, in the 6-2 he will block defensive tackle. Onside guard must know that his technique for blocking the defensive tackle is to gain *width* not depth.

Tackles

Like the center and the guard, the tackle has subtle details to be aware of also. As mentioned before, the offside tackle has to make a mental note about the slow development of the sprint-draw (14-15). There are other mental notes to be aware of. In the 5-2 Eagle as shown below, the offensive tackle now has the same technique as the guards in the sprint-draw (14-15). (See Diagram 7-24.) In the sprint-out passes (Green 14-15-18-19) the tackles have different responsibilities as shown in Chapter 2. Sprint-out run requires great lateral movement if confronted with 5-2 Eagle defense. Tackles, considering the myriad of defensive combinations, have very little to adjust to when blocking the sprint series.

Diagram 7-24: Right 14 5-2 Eagle

The techniques for blocking in the sprint series are described in detail in Chapter 2. The responsibilities of sprint-pass blocking, pass routes, and skilled positions are detailed in the preceding chapters. Yet, there are significant rules to remember.

1. Never use the sprint-draw in goal-line situations or your own end zone. When most defenses are in a goal-line situation, they must gamble and be somewhat reckless in attacking the offense. The defense tries to force the big mistake. Therefore, because of the slow development in executing the sprint-draw, the possibilities of a loss in four down territory is increased.
2. Sprint-out combinations are excellent in goal-line situations. With three threats to the outside, two receivers or the QB

turning upfield and running, the pressure created on the defensive perimeter is tremendous.

3. Sprint-draw pass is only effective if the run (sprint-draw) has been used often. The sprint-draw must sequence to the sprint-draw pass and vice versa. If a 5-2 LB'er is not shown the total development of the sprint series, the LB'er will be ignoring his false keys and the continuity of the offense will be slowed down. If the LB'er is not giving any respect to the QB's sprint-out by only playing the run, the sprint-draw pass to the outside receiver or his hook will be clear all during the game.

4. Use motion to diagnose the defense and to force the defense to play in a pre-determined manner.

5. Sequence your sprint series to the rest of your offense. If off-tackle is being vulnerable because of certain events, attack that vulnerability with sequential off-power plays that still appear to be sprint series oriented.

6. Sprint-draw is most effective against 4-4 defenses or 4-3 when using the twins formation to the side of play. With outside linebacker forced to play outside responsibility, a natural running lane is created for RB.

Sprint series is an offense in itself. But if a coach takes plays at random and expects results, he will be disappointed. The sprint series must be integrated in your total offensive philosophy completely. As to being multiple-motion, the integration of sequencing offenses becomes more difficult for defenses to react and adjust when confronting offenses that "appear" totally different each time.

8

Implementing the Veer in the
Multiple-Motion I Offense

A true veer attack requires a total commitment by your football staff and players. By total commitment, a football program must be veer not only in the make-up of practices, but also in its confidence in running the veer to win. A true veer attack, once committed, is an offense that cannot be junked in mid-season by a coaching staff and hope to maintain a cohesiveness for offensive consistency. The veer requires constant repetition in mesh points, pitch-outs, reading keys in the defensive line, etc., to maintain a precision-like timing that is necessary for outstanding veer play.

The *Multiple-Motion I Offense* borrows from the veer philosophy, but never attempts to run a true veer attack as related to drills and offensive selection of personnel. The "veer look" is used only to maintain the disguise of looking complicated to the defense, but remaining simple to the players. If an offense runs a variation of the veer, the defense must prepare to stop a true veer attack regardless whether the offense is true veer or not. Because of this defensive preparation for the veer, the *Multiple-Motion I Offense* utilizes the veer as part of its multiple attack. Moreover, the blocking for the veer is so simple that an offensive line can maintain a superior psychological edge because of its "many blocking schemes."

How does an offense borrow from the veer? The key to successful veer play is the ability of the quarterback to read the defense and decide to give, run, or pitch. If the decision to do these three items are taken away from the quarterback and each veer play is designed to go to a specific area regardless of the defensive scheme, the dependence on quarterback reading ability is cancelled. Instead of drilling veer reads, the offense only mirrors veer plays with pre-determined assignments. Granted, the very ingredient that makes veer attacks explode—the ability to run where there is no defense—is missing. But also missing is the predictable offense and its tendencies for defenses to prepare against. Because the *Multiple-Motion I Offense* pre-determines the three basic veer plays, little offensive time is spent in perfecting these plays. But what about the defense? Do they spend a *little* time in preparing for pitch man, dive back, containment of quarterback, etc.? *Of course not.* What if the defense knows that the offense is not reading their defensive line on the veer, will they prepare any less for stopping the potency of the veer? No, because pre-determined veer plays can strike just as deadly if no defensive preparation has been used.

VEER RUNS

All of the veer runs in the *Multiple-Motion I Offense* are run from the I. The philosophy for using the I instead of the split-back is that proper pitch relationship can be maintained easier by emphasizing I formations. Moreover, the I formation ties in to the same offensive package that the sprint series employs. (See Diagrams 8-1, 8-2, and 8-3.)

ON TACKLE:	Block 1st man inside, on or off the LOS.
ON GUARD:	Block 1.
CENTER:	Block onside gap.
OFF GUARD:	Block onside gap.
OFF TACKLE:	Block onside gap if man in gap; otherwise safety.
Y:	Block force vs 4 deep; otherwise block 1st LBer inside.
X:	Block middle ⅓.
Z:	Block outside ⅓.
DIVE BACK:	Run outside hip of guard; pressure-take ball. (None—fake.)
FLARE BACK:	Sprint to pitch relation.
QUARTERBACK ACTION AND ALERTS:	D.L. action, mesh with dive-back, fake option.

In Diagram 8-1, the onside LB'er will be double-teamed by the onside guard and tackle. The nose guard will be blocked by the center. If the center cannot block the nose guard, the veer rules will adjust so that nose guard will be double-teamed by the center and onside guard. This leaves the (No. 1 man) onside LB'er for the onside tackle.

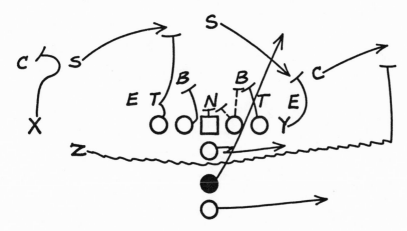

Diagram 8-1: Twins-Right 232 Veer

In Diagram 8-2, the 4-3 defensive tackle will be double-teamed by the onside guard and tackle. The center blocks the middle LB'er. It is very important for the center to step through the playside gap in pursuing the middle LB'er. The reason being that the center cannot allow any penetration through his playside gap. If he doesn't cover his playside gap, the mesh between the quarterback and fullback will be destroyed causing a complete breakdown in the timing of the play.

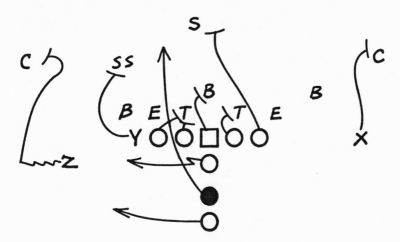

Diagram 8-2: Left 133 Veer

Diagram 8-3 illustrates the very specific rules of the inside veer. The onside tackle blocks his rule: first man inside on or off the LOS. The onside guard, however, doesn't help the tackle because the defensive

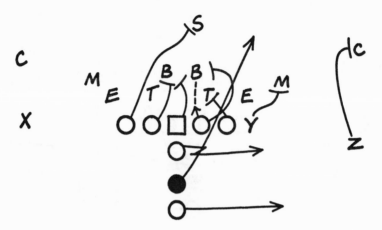

Diagram 8-3: Right 32 Veer

tackle is not No. 1 man. The onside LB'er is. The onside guard must fold block around the onside tackle's block to have any chance. In case the onside LB'er scrapes or slants to the inside while the onside guard is folding around, the center should be able to pick up any stunts because he is stepping through playside gap towards the onside LB'er.

The 32-33 Veer gives the offensive linemen an opportunity to "tee off" with their new approach in blocking the veer. This inside veer creates adjustments by the defense unless the defensive tackle on the onside is staying home and playing tough to the inside. If this occurs, the 34-35 Veer will be used to make the defensive tackle more aware of defensive responsibilities. (See Diagrams 8-4 and 8-5.)

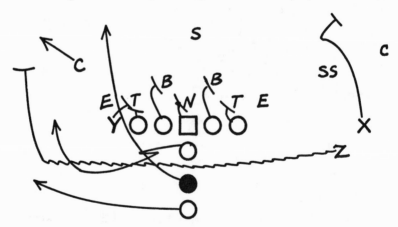

Diagram 8-4: Twins-Left 135 Veer

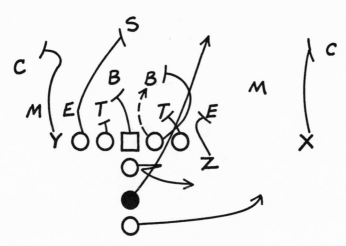

Diagram 8-5: Black-Left 34 Veer

ON TACKLE:	Block 2.
ON GUARD:	Block 1 (pull if you have to).
CENTER:	Block 0; off-side.
OFFENSIVE GUARD:	Block 1 over or outside; otherwise 2 ("If").
OFFENSIVE TACKLE:	Block 2 over or outside; otherwise 3 ("If").
Y:	Block 3 on or inside; otherwise, double team 2.
X:	Block middle ⅓.
Z:	Block outside ⅓.
DIVE BACK:	Dive over inside leg of tackle; quarterback will press ball on give.
FLARE BACK:	Sprint to pitch relationship.
QUARTERBACK ACTION AND ALERTS:	D.L. action mesh with dive-back; fake the option.

The Split 4-4 defense has become increasingly popular in striving to stop veer attacks. The *Multiple-Motion I Offense's* philosophy is to make defenses predictable. The 4-4 defense and its 3-deep secondary has been successful in coping with the veer. But, the split 4-4 defense is extremely vulnerable to the multiplicity of the *Multiple-Motion I Offense* and specifically its sprint series which is detailed in Chapter 7.

The 38-39 Veer is the pre-determined pitch. Naturally, the pitch is designed from a read factor by the quarterback. But, the 38-39 veer is only designed to confuse the defense into thinking that the offense has a complete veer package. (See Diagrams 8-6 and 8-7.)

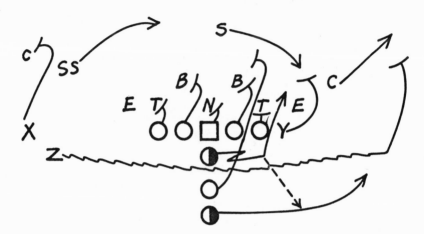

Diagram 8-6: Twins-Right 238 Veer

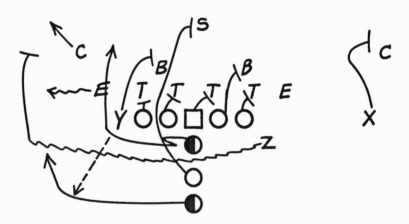

Diagram 8-7: Black-Left 139 Veer

ON TACKLE:	Block 2.
ON GUARD:	Block 1.
CENTER:	Block 0; off-side.
OFF GUARD:	Block 1 over or outside; otherwise 2 ("If").
OFF TACKLE:	Block 2 over or outside; otherwise 3 ("If").
	Block force vs. 4 deep; otherwise 3.

X:	Block Middle ⅓.
Z:	Block outside ⅓.
DIVE BACK:	Run outside hip of guard, fake, block 1st man to show.
FLARE BACK:	Sprint to pitch relation.
QUARTERBACK ACTION AND ALERTS:	D.L. action, fake to dive back, and option end.

38-39 Veer to X's Side (Split-End)

The rules for 38-39 Veer to (X's) side are identical to 38-39 Veer to (Y's) side except for one rule. The onside LB'er is not blocked. The reason is that the inside path of the fullback and the center scooping to his inside gap will keep the LB'er occupied. The onside guard pulls to split end's side to create a running lane for the quarterback. (Although the play is a pre-determined pitch, the quarterback still has the option of running.) The onside guard's block will hinge on two developments: if the defensive end comes across, the guard will kick him out with the quarterback running inside of it; if the defensive end sits and plays a soft technique, the guard will continue running to get an outside approach on the defensive end. (See Diagrams 8-10 and 8-11.)

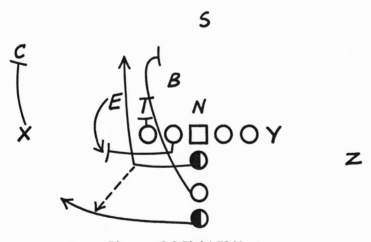

Diagram 8-8 Right 39 Veer

The key factor in running the 38-39 Veer to split-end's side is to put pressure on the defensive end to react. If the defensive end plays soft on his look of the veer, (X) will change his stalk-block and crackback on the defensive end. This leaves the defense with a cornerback playing deep

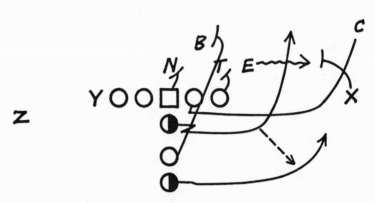

Diagram 8-9: Left 38 Veer (Def. end is
playing soft, therefore, X's rules
will be changed to crackback)

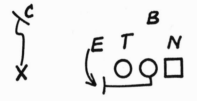

Diagram 8-10: 38-39 Veer (QB will run inside)

Diagram 8-11: 38-39 Veer (X has option of blocking def. end
or cornerback)

and a monster from an inside position versus an offensive guard and
running back. Any time a back can operate with space in a vertical
fashion along with a lead blocker, pressure mounts on the backs of the
defensive perimeter. To emphasize again, the purpose of the veer in the
Multiple-Motion I Offense is not to be a finesse offense. It's only role is to
appear as a true veer and make defenses adjust to it.

If defensive pursuit from the LB'er play becomes too great on the
38-39 Veer to split-end side, a sucker veer will be called. The sucker veer

is simply a give to the fullback with an angle by the fullback towards the inside leg of onside guard. (See Diagram 8-12.)

The rules are identical to the normal 38-39 Veer. The only exceptions are the path taken by the fullback and the onside guard pulling. This play is not a bread and butter veer play. The purpose is to serve notice for respecting the fullback dive. If respect is not given, the fullback can bust for a long one.

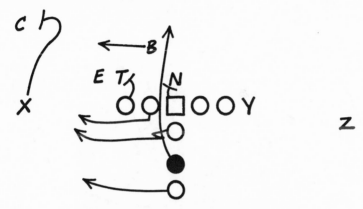

Diagram 8-12: Right 39 Sucker Veer

SPECIAL VEER OPTIONS

Remaining consistent in attempting to confuse the defense and appear as a true veer attack, the *Multiple-Motion I Offense* uses two options off its "veer" look. Both options are used to take advantage of defensive weaknesses.

First is the 28-29 option. This option is whereby the quarterback attacks the defensive end directly and/or runs with the ball or pitches to the tailback who has the fullback as his lead blocker. (This play can be run also with a near-backfield formation in which the fullback will carry and the tailback will be the lead blocker.) (See Diagrams 8-13 and 8-14.)

ON TACKLE:	Block 2.
ON GUARD:	Block 1.
CENTER:	Block 0; off-side.
OFF GUARD:	Block 1 over or outside; otherwise 2 ("If").
OFF TACKLE:	Block 2 over or outside; otherwise 3 ("If").
Y:	Block 3 on or inside; otherwise, double team 2.

X:	Block middle ⅓.
Z:	Crack back block on force man.
LEAD BACK:	Sprint to junction block on corner back.
FLARE BACK:	Counter step, sprint to pitch relationship.
QUARTERBACK ACTION & ALERTS:	Alabama action, option the defense end.

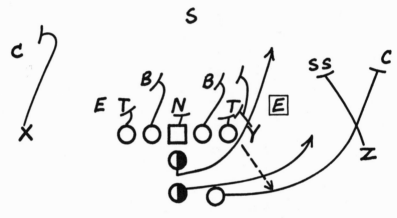

Diagram 8-13: Near-Right 28 Option

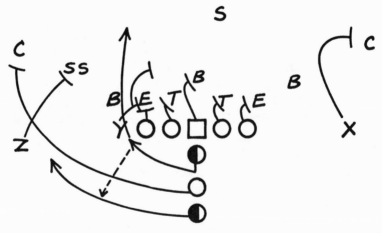

Diagram 8-14: Left 29 Option

As described in Chapter 4, the Alabama quarterback action is a drop-back of 2-3 yards. As the quarterback retreats, he clutches the ball chest-high with two hands as if he is going to pass. This movement by the quarterback allows the LB'ers to key pass and move backwards. The back-pedaling by the LB'ers allows the pitch or the run by the quarterback to have less inside defensive pursuit. The key technique of the 28-29 option is attacking the defensive end (No. 3 man in 7-man fronts, No. 4 in 8-man fronts) by the quarterback. There must be a quick decision on the quarterback's part to either pitch or run. This quick decision can only be made easier if the quarterback runs directly at the defensive end and makes the defensive man commit. If the end comes at the quarterback, the pitch is made automatically. It doesn't matter if the end is 3-4 yards away from the quarterback, for the defensive end's shoulders are turned into the offensive backfield, and the tailback will have the angle in the foot race.

Running the 28-29 option to the split-end side requires very few adjustments. The biggest adjustment is that the defensive tackle will not be double-teamed because there is no tight-end. This adjustment means that the onside tackle must be able to block one-on-one with the defensive tackle. This block doesn't have to be a blow-out, knock-'em down affair. The 28-29 play only requires the quarterback to be able to run in a direct line at the No. 3 man or No. 4 man. If this path is obstructed with defensive pressure from the defensive tackle, the play's timing will result in poor yardage.

Another adjustment to be made is that the split-end crackbacks on the LB'er. Crackback rules and technique for wide receivers as described in Chapter 6 are vital. The fullback again has a junction block on the cornerback and must be able to block under control. (See Diagram 8-15.)

The second option employed by the *Multiple-Motion I Offense* is a sequential play off the 28-29 option which is designed to take advantage

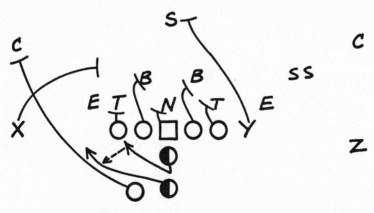

Diagram 8-15: Far-Right 29 Option

of defensive pursuit. This option is simply called Counter 28-29 and is always run to split-end's side to simplify assignments. (See Diagram 8-16.)

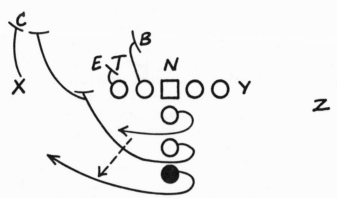

Diagram 8-16: Right-Counter 28 (FB blocks def. end
if end is staying home)

ON TACKLE:	Block 2.
ON GUARD:	Block 1.
CENTER:	Block 0; off-side.
OFF GUARD:	Block 1 over or outside; otherwise 2 ("If").
OFF TACKLE:	Block 2 over or outside: otherwise 3 ("If").
Y:	Block outside man, release the middle ⅓.
X:	Block outside ⅓.
Z:	Block middle ⅓.
LEAD BACK:	Sprint to junction block on corner back (360° turn prior to making junction block); or block defensive end.
FLARE BACK:	Sprint to pitch relationship (360° turn prior to making junction block).
QUARTERBACK ACTION AND ALERTS:	Spin pivot and pitch immediately.

NOTE: Counter option is always run opposite of numbers called.

There is no crackback by (X). The reasons are that movement by the backs in the wrong direction and success from the regular 28-29 option will insure poor defensive pursuit by the LB'ers. Because of the crackback cancellation, the fullback will either block the defensive end or double-team with (X) on the corner. Notice that the fullback has the option of blocking defensive end, whereas in the 28-29 option the quarterback options the No. 3 or No. 4 man. The quarterback always pitches on the counter 28-29 option. Because of the quarterback's spin pivot which allows very little time to recognize defensive pressure, the counter option calls for the quarterback to pitch immediately to the tailback after completing spin and completing first step towards split-end's side.

VEER PASSES

All veer passes are play-action with the color green used as the signal for pass instead of run. Veer passes are green 32-33, Green 34-35, and Green 28-29 option.

The Green 32-33 veer pass play is designed to take advantage of a closing strong-safety or force in a defense. This play requires all backs to run their designed 32-33 veer. Linemen block their 80 pass blocking rules (Chapter 3). The quarterback rides the fullback and then drifts back looking for (Y) on his outside release. The quarterback must wait and give (Y) time to get clear. Moreover, the pass must be to (Y's) outside shoulder for (Y) is splitting the seam between the free safety and cornerback. If (Y) is not open, the quarterback dumps ball to tailback in flat area who has run his pitch-technique first. (See Diagrams 8-17 and 8-18.)

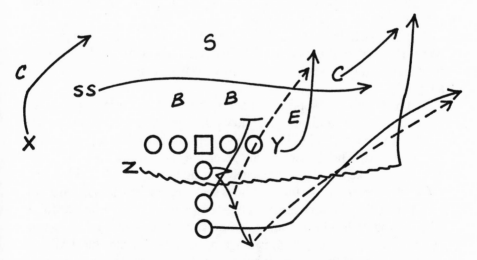

Diagram 8-17: Black-Right Green 232 Veer

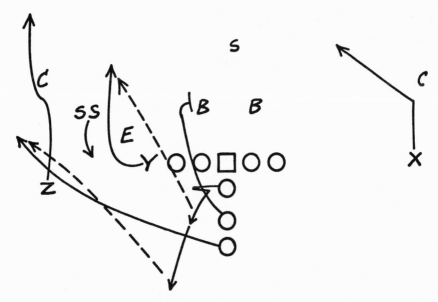

Diagram 8-18: Left-Green 33 Veer

The Green 34-35 Veer pass play is similar to Green 32-33 Veer. The difference in Green 34-35 is that (Y) does not release outside but inside and runs a diagonal pattern. Both backs run their outside veer techniques with the tailback running his flat pattern after showing the possibility of a pitch. The fullback, however, has to block the defensive end and not fake carrying the ball. When the quarterback pulls out the ball on the outside veer mesh point, he must be able to retreat and plant 3-4 yards behind mesh point. (See Diagram 8-19.)

The quarterback reads the backside LB'er to (Y's) diagonal passing point. If the space is not created by (X's) route, the quarterback looks for back in flat and passes if open. If strong safety is near, throw the ball away.

The Green 28-29 option is a halfback pass. The quarterback shows no Alabama action and only gives down the line action for 2-3 steps, then pitches to the tailback. The fullback sprint blocks (Chapter 5) the defensive end. The tailback, upon receiving the ball, doesn't run for a few steps to fake run. He immediately sets up behind onside tackle's area 5-7 yards deep and looks for (Z) who is showing crackback route on force and then curling behind corner. This pass play will only be successful if corner support has been coming up quickly for contain. There are no other receivers but (Z). If (Z) isn't open, the tailback runs for daylight. He doesn't throw the ball away because he hasn't been coached to throw 40 yard passes away. (See Diagram 8-20.)

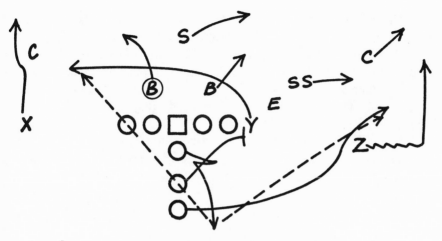

Diagram 8-19: Right-Green 234 Veer

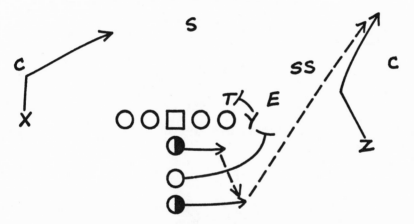

Diagram 8-20: Right-Green 28 Option

NOTE: The ball should be passed to (Z's) outside shoulder to escape from free safety's play.

BASE RUNNING AND PASSING PLAYS

The base series is introduced in the veer chapter because they mirror the veer plays. Only the offensive blocking is not veer but base blocking. Again this sequencing is designed for the offense so it can be multiple but simple.

Base running plays and passes are the lead series and fullback dives in the *Multiple-Motion I Offense*. The reason for describing the lead and fullback dive plays as base is that these plays require very little blocking adjustments by the offensive line. Moreover, base is a term frequently used by coaches to denote rule blocking for the offensive line. Chapter 2 describes in detail the adjustments of line play for running the lead plays against various defenses. However, the following plays are given without the word base and are used within the nomenclature that has been given in this book. The word base is never used in the play calling. If nothing is added to the plays, base is automatic.

The 22-23 Lead has been described and diagramed in earlier chapters. But the reason for running the 22-23 Lead and when to run it have not been discussed. To review the play again see Diagrams 8-21 and 8-22.

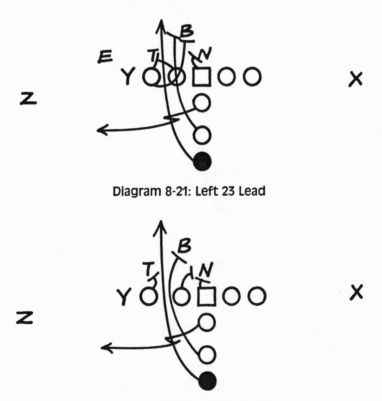

Diagram 8-21: Left 23 Lead

Diagram 8-22: Left 23 Lead

The lead is not a finesse football play. The 22-23 Lead is designed to put pressure on the LB'er to fill and shed the isolation blocker, the fullback. The play has a chance to be more successful if the center can handle the nose guard by himself. If the center cannot handle the nose guard and needs help, the defense can read the play easier and squeeze the running lane down. (See Diagram 8-22.)

The 22-23 Lead play can be disguised with the use of motion and multiple formations. (See Diagrams 8-23, 8-24, and 8-25.)

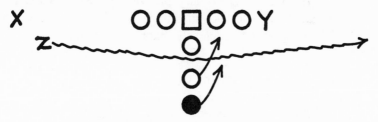

Diagram 8-23: Twins-Right 222 Lead

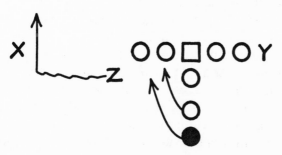

Diagram 8-24: Black-Right 123 Lead

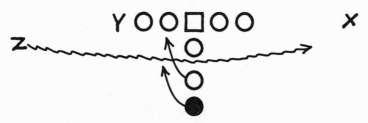

Diagram 8-25: Left 223 Lead

Football coaches know that good interior defenses should ignore the formations and usage of motion. But do they? With the multiple use of the *Multiple-Motion I Offense,* the 22-23 Lead can be run from so many different looks that scouting reports can get no tendencies. Why and when should you run the lead? The lead should be run if only for one reason—it makes the defense respect the middle of the line. Offenses must be able to attack anywhere to be successful. The 22-23 Lead not only attacks the middle, but is a great sequential play for other features of the *Multiple-Motion I Offense*—counter, sprint-draw, traps, and the veer. The sequencing of plays is so important in making offensive decisions as to what you run.

The 22-23 Lead certainly should be called to make the defense respect the middle. But the primary purpose of the 22-23 Lead is not only for respect but also to take advantage of defensive weaknesses.

The following is a list of defensive happenings that could give reason for calling the 22-23 Lead:

1. LB'er's playing unusually deep.
2. Nose guard slanting to tight-end side only, two man receiver side, away from motion. Anything that makes the defense predictable will be extremely vulnerable to lead.
3. LB'er sliding to outside when motion is to his side.
4. Defensive tackles that play too wide on offensive tackles.
5. Defensive tackles are looping to tight-end side.
6. Middle LB'er on 4-3 defense who is playing deep.

Many defenses are giving a split 4 look to combat the veer attacks. The 22-23 Lead is extremely successful against these defensive looks. Moreover, because of this success, the I formation instead of the split-back becomes a stronger backfield formation for running the veer.

Diagram 8-26 illustrates how to utilize a "simple" lead play against the ever popular split-4 defense.

The tight-end (Y) must release outside to give the LB'er a fake key. This outside release makes the LB'er give width to the offense because he

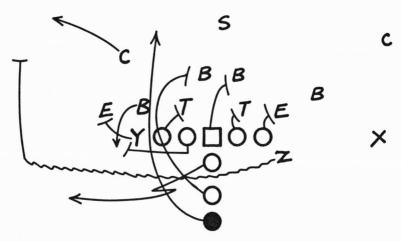

Diagram 8-26: Black-Left 123 Lead

must step outside with (Y) and give respect to the flat as a possible pass play. This width, if only one step, gives the onside guard the great blocking angle needed to block the outside LB'er. Moreover, width is created for the P.O.A. because of the great blocking angle that the offensive tackle has on the defensive tackle. The fullback blocks the onside LB'er. If the onside LB'er fires through guard's pulling lane, the fullback should be able to pick him up easily. The defensive end is not blocked because the onside guard's block on outside LB'er should wall off any pursuit from the defensive end if he is playing normal technique.

This one adjustment by the offense enables the 22 Lead to be an explosive play. Granted, blocking rules have been changed to block this defense. But the philosophy of the *Multiple-Motion I Offense* is to recognize defenses and block accordingly. The tight-end's (Y's) rule on 22-23 Lead is to block widest man. But against the split 4, (Y) must be able to adjust and give the fake key. The offensive team's ability to adjust and react to defensive situations will determine offensive consistency.

The 24-25 Lead is similar to the 22-23 Lead except for the P.O.A. and line blocking schemes. The 24-25 Lead is designed to take advantage of one thing—the ability of a defensive end to squeeze an off-tackle running play. (See Diagram 8-27.)

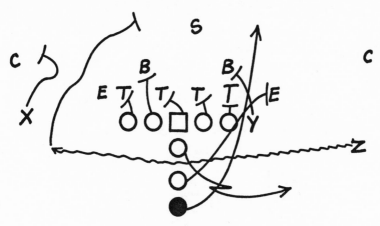

Diagram 8-27: Right 124 Lead

The blocking rules for 24-25 Lead are identical to the base blocking rules of 22-23 Lead, except for (Y) and fullback. Tight-end will always double-team with the onside offensive tackle unless three man is inside of the tight-end. The fullback blocks the defensive end instead of the inside linebacker in the 24-25 Lead.

Can the inside LB'er and defensive end stop the play? Will the inside LB'er be able to escape the block of the onside guard and scrape to the off-tackle hole? Will the defensive end be able to take on the fullback and constrict the running lane of the tailback? If these questions cannot be answered positively by the defense, the offense should never stop running the 24-25 Lead. Furthermore, if the onside defensive tackle is pinching in or can be blocked one-on-one by the onside tackle, the tight-end (Y) can pick up the onside LB'er on a combo block technique. (See Diagram 8-28.)

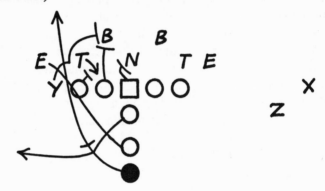

Diagram 8-28: Twins-Left 25 Lead

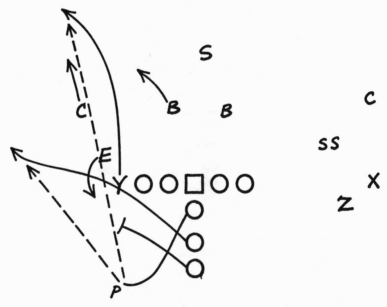

Diagram 8-29: Twins-Left Green 25

Green 24-25 is a great example of sequencing offensive plays. Defensive end play is the key concept for the Green 24-25 pass play. If the defensive end is crashing hard for constriction of running lane when the 24-25 Lead has been called, and the LB'er is pursuing inside to the off-tackle hole, the Green 24-25 will be successful. The Green 24-25 is always run to the opposite of defensive secondary's strength. The reason is to attack the flat where the weakside LB'er or defensive end have flat responsibilities. Since 24-25 Lead has made the defensive end conscious of the fullback blocking him, the defensive end play should be weak against Green 24-25. Moreover, onside LB'er will be scraping to the off-tackle hole and will have poor pursuit on fullback in flat. (See Diagram 8-29.)

NOTE: Quarterback reads fullback first, if covered, (Y) is open on flag route.

Every football team has some play where the fullback dives. 32-33 run is exactly that. This play is always run from I backfield formation. The technique of the backfield play is similar to the 32-33 Veer. The difference for the 32-33 is the line blocking. Everyone on the line blocks base. The one exception to this base blocking scheme is the 4-4 defense. The defensive tackle and LB'er cannot be blocked effectively by the onside guard-tackle fold blocking. Why? The fullback gets to the hole too quickly from his fullback alignment. To overcome this problem with 4-4 defensive tackle, the onside guard-tackle double-team the defensive tackle. (See Diagram 8-30.) The onside LB'er will not be blocked. Double-team by onside guard-tackle will wall off LB'er pursuit. If outstanding LB'er play is occuring, 32-33 run will be difficult to succeed. The 32-33, however, is not designed for touch-down purposes, but short yardage situations and to help sequence offensive plays from 32-33 look.

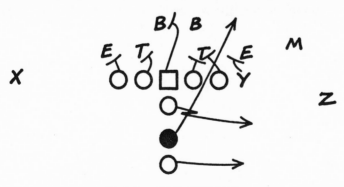

Diagram 8-30: Right 32

Green 32-33 is a play-action pass with the tight-end (Y) as the primary receiver. The quarterback looks for (Y) after faking a 32-33 run with the fullback, hoping to lure the onside LB'er in. (Y) releases inside and looks immediately for the quick pass. If (Y) is covered, the quarterback retreats deep from his mesh point with the fullback and looks for the tailback running a flare route. (See Diagram 8-31.)

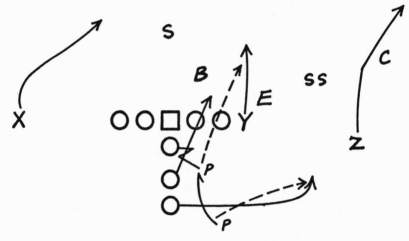

Diagram 8-31: Right-Green 32

The Green 32-33 play-action pass is very successful in goal-line defenses and short yardage situations. The 6-5 defense is very vulnerable to the (Y) route on Green 32-33. However, the flare route run by the tailback can be dangerous to the defense if the tailback doesn't remember to run toward the flag if goal-line is near. The reason is that (Z) cannot run his up route because of lack of room, therefore (Z) adjusts his pattern to a hook, hoping to lure the corner inside. (See Diagram 8-32.)

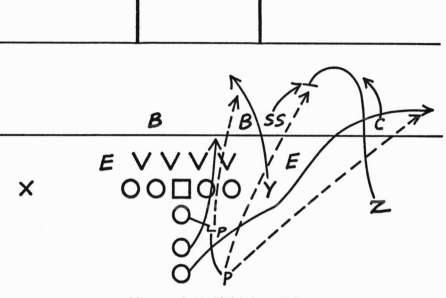

Diagram 8-32: Right-Green 32

9

Coaching the Special Series
in the Multiple-Motion I

TAILBACK AND FULLBACK TRAP

The trap play implemented with the *Multiple-Motion I Offense* is unique in that either the tailback or fullback can be the ball carrier without adding or changing any nomenclature. Simply a third digit is added to indicate the tailback trap, whereas if a third digit is not added, the fullback carries the ball. Moreover, the line blocking remains constant regardless of who is carrying the ball.

The 30-31 Trap, like most traps, works most effectively against even defenses. Even defenses present an easier blocking angle for the trapping guard. Furthermore, even defenses have a more difficult time reacting to trap blocking techniques because the trap occurs quicker than when being run against an odd defense. (See Diagrams 9-1, 9-2, and 9-3.)

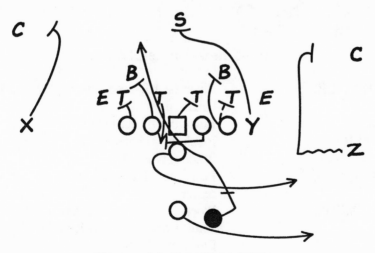

Diagram 9-1: Near-Right 131 Trap

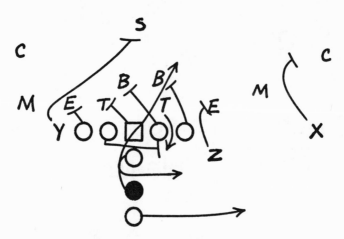

Diagram 9-2: Black-Left 30 Trap

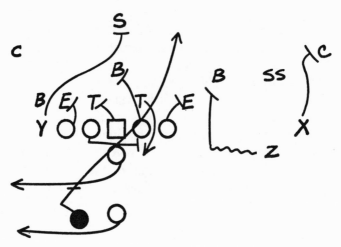

Diagram 9-3: Near-Twins Left 130 Trap

ON TACKLE:	Block 1st LB'er on side of play; vs. 6-2, block out.
ON GUARD:	Block 0; offside; turn out.
CENTER:	Block down lineman in off-guard's area; if none, block 0.
OFF GUARD:	Pull, trap 1st down linemen beyond center.
OFF TACKLE:	Block 1st man head-up to outside.
Y:	Slam widest man; block middle ⅓.
X:	Block middle ⅓.

Z:	Block middle ⅓.
DIVE BACK:	Step for center's offside foot, cut just inside guard's trap.
FLARE BACK:	Sprint to pitch relationship *away* from hole.
QUARTERBACK ACTION & ALERTS:	D.L. action away from hole called, hand-off as deep as you can, carry out fake.

Diagrams 9-1, 9-2, and 9-3 demonstrate the weakness or vulnerability of even defenses. To exploit these weaknesses, it is paramount for the ball carrier to read the trap block correctly. When the tailback carries the ball (9-1 and 9-3), the angle of the tailback's running path allows a much easier view to see the trap block than the fullback's path (9-2). As most trap plays, the 30-31 trap works best when the defense is surprised. We attempt to exploit our traps in passing situations, especially if there has been a fierce pass rush. Passing situations help to complement the 30-31 Trap with surprise.

When defensive teams are expecting a pass and the 30-31 Trap is called, a good run usually results because of the surprise element. But, many defensive teams like to stunt on passing situations, which can create confusion for the offensive linemen unless they remember to treat LB'er's as down linemen when stunting is apparent. (See Diagrams 9-4 and 9-5.)

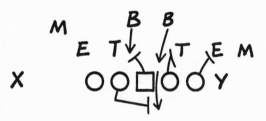

Diagram 9-4: Trap vs. Stunting LB'ers

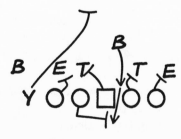

Diagram 9-5: Trap vs. Stunting LB'ers

Although trap plays generally are more effective against even defenses, the 30-31 Trap can be run quite successfully versus odd defenses such as the popular 5-2 defense. The success, however, depends on slight adjustments at the POA. These adjustments are vital to successful 30-31 Traps. (See Diagrams 9-6, 9-7, and 9-8.)

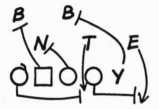

Diagram 9-6: 5-2 Defense vs. Trap

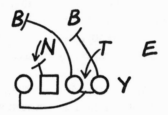

Diagram 9-7: 5-2 Slant Defense

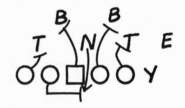

Diagram 9-8: Offset 5-2 vs. Trap

Diagram 9-6 illustrates the concern that the 5-2 defensive tackle poses for the 30-31 Trap. If the onside offensive tackle blocks his normal rule for the 30-31 Trap, the defensive tackle will close the trap hole. (See Diagram 9-9.)

The defensive tackle in most 5-2 defenses has been coached to react inside when the offensive tackle comes down inside on the LB'er. This inside rush by the defensive tackle makes the trap block by the guard a most difficult chore. Therefore, to make the defensive tackle react

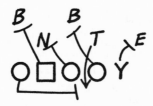

Diagram 9-9: 5-2 Defensive Tackle Reads

outside instead of inside, the offensive tackle and tight-end exchange assignments. The offensive tackle steps back and to the outside to influence the defensive tackle to read a false key. (See Diagram 9-10.) This false key enables the trapping guard to have a great blocking angle on the defensive tackle. The tight-end closes down quickly on the onside LB'er. The defensive end is screened out by the defensive tackle being trapped. If the defensive end pursues to the outside, the offensive tackle will have an easy block on him.

Diagram 9-7 displays a coaching technique that must be reinforced constantly to the players if a 5-2 slant is going to be trapped consistently. The center's rules on all 30-31 Traps are to block 0 to offside. In addition, it is the offside guard's rule to block 0 only when confronted with a 5-2 defense. But, if the nose guard slants away from the off-side guard's blocking angle, the rules are no longer valid. Therefore, the offside guard and center must be drilled into reacting to this maneuver.

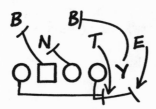

Diagram 9-10: False Keys for 5-2 Defensive Tackle

The offside guard when blocking the nose guard must continue on to the backside LB'er if the nose guard disappears. Of course, the center in going through the nose guard to block the backside LB'er must continue to rip block the nose guard if his slant is in the center's angle toward the LB'er. (See Diagram 9-11.)

Offset 5-2 defense doesn't present a problem for the 30-31 Trap. The nose guard becomes the trap man since he is the first down lineman past the center. Even though the offset doesn't present any real blocking problems, the recognition of this defense is a problem for the line because of its unfamiliarity to football teams. One item that is of concern in blocking the offset is that the offside offensive tackle must scramble quickly to pick-off the offside defensive tackle. Because the defensive tackle can read the pulling guard easily, the pursuit by the defensive tackle can destroy the timing of the 30-31 Trap. Therefore, the offside offensive tackle must react quickly and chop the defensive tackle down.

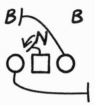

Diagram 9-11: Slant Defense vs. Trap

TRAP OPTION

The 30-31 Trap Option is designed to take advantage of odd fronts such as the 5-2 defense that react so quickly to trap blocking. The 30-31 Trap Option is only successful if the 30-31 Trap has been sequenced along with the option. This football play should be utilized only if it is an integral part of the offense.

Diagram 9-12 illustrates the complete play along with the options available to the quarterback. Responsibilities in running the trap option versus the 30-31 Trap are altered only for (Y), trapping guard, and the quarterback. Everyone else blocks his normal trap rules:

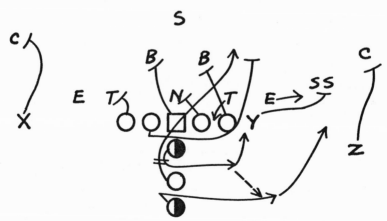

Diagram 9-12: Right 30 Trap Option 5-2 Defense

Y: Outside release and block strong safety or force.

QUARTERBACK: Lead through behind guard's block or pitch if defensive end pinches in.

The key technique for successful trap options is that the quarterback must understand and read the defensive end's reaction. If the defensive end shows any signs that he is closing in on the pulling trap guard, the pitch to the tailback is automatic. (See Diagram 9-13.)

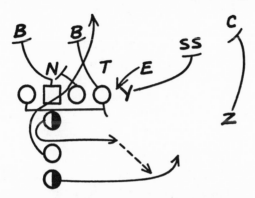

Diagram 9-13: Reading Trap-Option Keys

However, if the defensive end maintains an option posture, the quarterback has a lead blocker (pulling guard) and a wide POA for running. The pulling trap guard in leading through the defensive tackle-end area must react to the defensive end's posture also. If the defensive end turns in when the quarterback runs, the guard never guesses if the defensive end is close enough or not. The guard simply blocks the first man to show as he runs by the defensive tackle who is expecting to be trap blocked. Naturally, if the defensive end is playing pitch, the guard will be able to recognize it immediately because of the natural width being created automatically by the defensive end. When this occurs, the guard is looking for people in the secondary. The onside LB'er should be occupied with the onside offensive tackle's block and the 30-31 Trap fake to the fullback.

COUNTER

The 40-41 Counter has been referred to in earlier chapters as the inside misdirection play of the *Multiple-Motion I Offense.* This football play is not unique to proponents of the I offense. However, as said in Chapter 2, the blocking schemes are varied and unique in employing the 40-41 Counter.

ON TACKLE:	Fold block 1 if LB'er; otherwise, block 2.
ON GUARD:	Block 1 if 1 is down; otherwise, block 2.
CENTER:	Block 0; off-side.
OFF GUARD:	Block 1 over or outside; otherwise 2 ("If").
OFF TACKLE:	Block 2 over or outside; otherwise 3 ("If").
Y:	Block out on 3; vs. 6-2, fold inside and block 3.
X:	Block middle ⅓.
Z:	Block middle ⅓.
DIVE BACK:	Run at outside hip of guard opposite hole and make hard fake.
BALL CARRIER:	Drop step; hit over guard reading block.
QUARTERBACK ACTION & ALERTS:	Counter action, fake to back away from hole, reach ball deep to ball carrier, hand-off, and continue fake.

The 40-41 Counter is sequenced off the lead series and is quite effective if backside defensive pursuit is not reading their keep properly, particularly the backside LB'er. In Diagram 9-14, the backside LB'er is

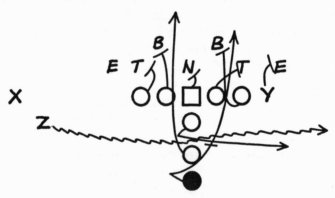

Diagram 9-14: Twins-Right 240 Counter

really the onside LB'er when exploiting defensive weaknesses. The press box coaches must recognize the backside LB'er's mistakes during the lead series for the 40-41 Counter to exploit this weakness on the onside LB'er. Defensive coaches constantly stress to their LB'er's to take a shuffle step or counter step when pursuit is away, so that they can react to misdirection plays. This maneuver for backside LB'er's is not difficult, but to train the mind to stay put is! The 40-41 Counter is designed to take advantage of backside LB'er's lack of mental discipline. (See Diagram 9-15 and 9-16.)

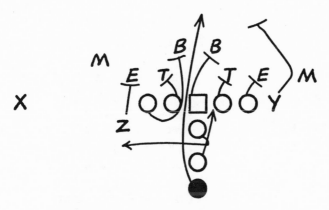

Diagram 9-15: Black-Left 41 Counter

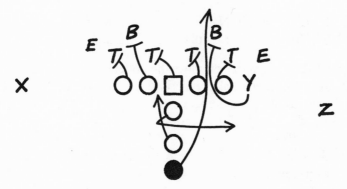

Diagram 9-16: Right 40 Counter

The 40-41 Counter is quite successful against goal-line defenses. The offensive blocking techniques, however, must be altered to gap blocking because of the tendency of goal-line defenses to rush many people in various directions. The *Multiple-Motion I Offense* utilizes the counter when operating inside the opponent's 10-yard line for one simple reason—defensive pursuit. The LB'ers and defensive linemen are coached to penetrate and pursue with reckless abandon—especially the LB'ers who can now forget their mental preparation of staying home because "their backs are against the wall." The 40-41 Counter simply uses the defensive pursuit ot its advantage by faking to the fullback and countering with the tailback. The simplicity of the counter and its importance to the total, overall offensive sequencing to the *Multiple-Motion I Offense* makes it a dangerous offensive weapon when attacking goal-line defenses.

TOSS

ON TACKLE:	Reach block playside gap.
ON GUARD:	Reach block playside gap.
CENTER:	Reach block playside gap.
OFF TACKLE:	Reach block playside gap.
OFF GUARD:	Reach block playside gap.
Y:	Reach block playside gap.
X:	Block middle ⅓.
Z:	Crack back on force man.
BACK:	Sprint to junction block corner-back.
BALL CARRIER:	Stay parallel to L.O.S. and read back's block.
QUARTERBACK ACTION AND ALERTS:	Reverse action, pitch 2-hand underhand plass—lead through guard-tackle hole.

Any offensive team that employs the I offense employs a variation of the 26-27 Toss. Southern Cal popularized the toss as "student body left or right." Regardless of the nomenclature tagged to the 26-27 Toss, it is still an outstanding football play and used very much in pro, college, or high school football.

The *Multiple-Motion I Offense* sequences the 26-27 Toss with several ideas in mind:

1. Run the defense sideline-to-sideline. (The bigger the opponent, the more you run it.)
2. To loosen the middle for traps, counters, etc.
3. Force the defensive backs to be *all-around* football players—can they shed blocks and make open-field tackles.
4. To set up the secondary for the home run ball—Green 26-27 Toss.

Can a defense run laterally? Can a defense be out-quicked? Can a defense tire? Will the secondary forget keys and force too quickly? Will defensive linemen be prepared for double-teams, traps, cross-blocking after being reached several times? The 26-27 toss is sequenced to probe these questions.

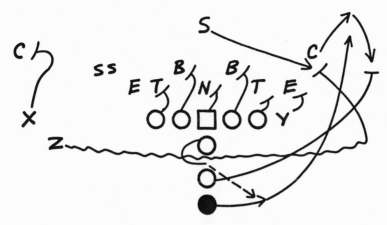

Diagram 9-17: Twins-Left 226 Toss

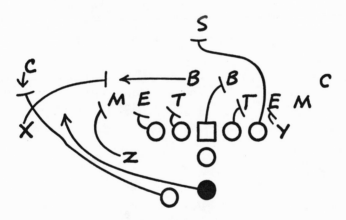

Diagram 9-18: Far-Black Right 27 Toss

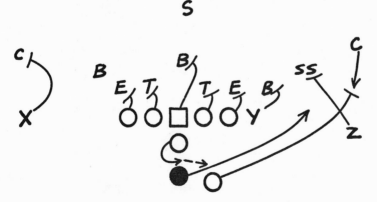

Diagram 9-19: Near-Right 26 Toss

Key defensive people in stopping the 26-27 Toss are the defensive end and cornerback. The cornerback must defeat the back's block and force the running back to the defensive inside. The defensive end must shed the tight-end's reach block and force the running back to the defensive inside pursuit. (See Diagram 9-20.)

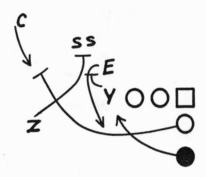

Diagram 9-20: Toss vs. Perimeter

Green 26-27 Toss and Green 26-27 Halfback Toss are designed to take advantage of the corner-back and defensive end if they are executing correctly. Of course, if they are not, "the" 26-27 Toss will be run until the defense can stop it. (See Diagrams 9-21 and 9-22.)

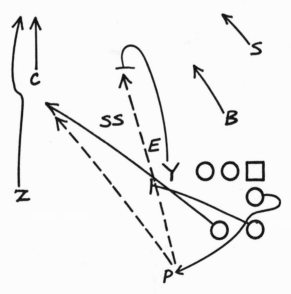

Diagram 9-21: Near-Left Green 27 Toss

Diagram 9-21 illustrates "Z" doing an up pattern, "Y" a hook to outside shoulder, and near running back a flat pattern. The quarterback fakes a toss pitch and rolls out reading the strong-safety's position. If the strong-safety slides to the outside, (Y) is open for the outside hook. The strong safety stays in position and attempts to play short zone, the quarterback passes to back on flat route. (Z's) up pattern is designed for clearing the passing areas for (Y) and the running back. The Green 26-27 Toss is sequenced off the 26-27 Toss based on the effectiveness of the defensive end's play on the 26-27 Toss. Why the defensive end? If the defensive end has been reacting well to (Y's) reach block on him and pursuing to near back's outside shoulder block, the defensive end presents two important ingredients for a successful Green 26-27 Toss:

1. Limited outside pass rush because of fake toss.
2. Clearer passing lane to (Y) on his hook.

Diagram 9-22 demonstrates the sequencing of the Green 26-27 Halfback Toss when the cornerback has been ignoring pass responsibilities and flying up for the 26-27 Toss. (Y) runs a square pattern and (Z) shows his crackback route on strong-safety and breaks to his flag route. The backfield technique is simply a toss to far-back (I formation is tailback) and back shows toss for 2-3 steps and stops to pass. The near back blocks defensive end. The Green 26-27 Halfback Toss is only successful against cornerbacks who are playing the toss too aggressively. If the free safety rolls to the outside ½ and is anywhere near (Z) on his route, the running back passes to (Y) on his square route.

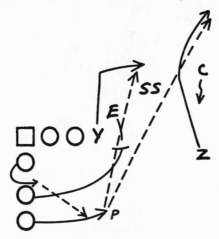

Diagram 9-22: Right-Green 26 HB Toss

DRAWS

The lead draw is a tremendous football play if running is comple-mented with a passing attack. The concept behind the lead draw is to run through a POA that has been partially created by the defense in its attempt to stop the offense on an "obvious passing situation." (See Diagrams 9-23 and 9-24.)

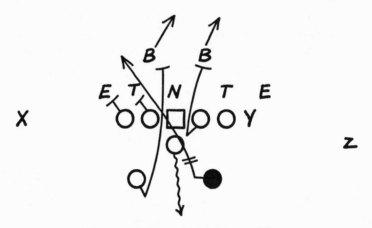

Diagram 9-23: Split-Right Lead Draw

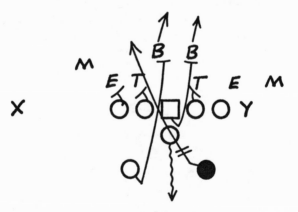

Diagram 9-24: Split-Right Lead Draw

ON TACKLE:	Block "If" rule.
ON GUARD:	Block "If" rule.
CENTER:	Block 0; off-side.
OFF GUARD:	Block "If" rule.

OFF TACKLE:	Block "If" rule.
Y:	Block middle ⅓.
Z:	Show pass route deep, then stalk block.
X:	Show pass route deep, then stalk block.
TAILBACK:	Crow-hop lead blocker through guard-center gap.
FULLBACK:	Slide to quarterback with inside arm up; maintain eyes downfield.
QUARTERBACK ACTION & ALERTS:	Back-pedal showing pass; inside hand-off to fullback, continue to back-pedal after hand-off showing pass.

NOTE: The lead draw is always run by the fullback to the same side.

The lead draw must be run from a split backfield to further disguise the look of a "passing formation." Moreover, the quarterback's back-pedalling and hand-off to the split-back is easier to execute when there is a split backfield formation. The non-carrying back in the split backfield is the lead blocker through the POA. This back must crow-hop to maintain timing with the quarterback's false cues and back running the ball. The key technique, however, with the lead back is to block anyone who shows in the onside guard-center's gap. Normally, the defense's pass rush creates a natural lane for both the lead blocker and the ball carrier and the lead back has a stalk block on the onside LB'er who dropped back on pass responsibilities. But, as in any football play, defenses do not always react the same. Therefore, the lead blocker must be prepared to have a collision with anyone that enters the POA.

Draw to "Z" (Flanker)

The *Multiple-Motion I Offense* uses the draw to (Z) as a play to take advantage of the defense when they are pursuing too aggressively on the sprint series. (See Diagrams 9-25, 9-26, and 9-27.)

ON TACKLE:	2 (except vs. 4-4, block inside LB'er with fold technique).
ON GUARD:	1 (except vs. 4-4, block tackle).
CENTER:	0; off-side.
OFF GUARD:	1 over or outside; otherwise 2 ("If").
OFF TACKLE:	2 over or outside; otherwise ("If").
Y:	Slam widest man—release block middle ⅓.
X:	Block middle ⅓.

Z:	Drop step open up to quarterback, look for hole over center.
FULLBACK:	Block 3 toward play.
TAILBACK:	Flare toward play.
QUARTERBACK ACTION & ALERTS:	Sprint-out technique to flat, hand-off to back while passing by—let fullback cross in front first.

The draw to (Z) is not a bread-butter type play. It is designed to do two things: surprise the defense and get the big run which is so demoralizing to any defense; if unsuccessful in regards to the big run, the draw to (Z) is successful in delaying backside pursuit when executing sprint-series plays. The *Multiple-Motion I Offense* runs the draw to (Z) as a part of a total offensive game plan. Regardless of yardage gained, the draw to (Z) has a purpose in offensive thinking if proper play sequencing has been employed.

In Diagram 9-25, the guards show pass for a one count then block the LB'ers. Showing pass false keys the LB'ers into dropping back for pass protection. The nose guard is blocked in the direction he is flowing. All the center must do is let the nose guard take a side and then use the nose guard's momentum against him. The tackles drive block their men and prevent inside penetration. If confronted with a 5-2 Eagle, the tackles would exchange with the guard's technique and show pass for a one count.

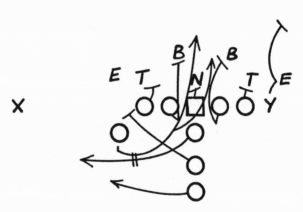

Diagram 9-25: Black-Right Draw to Z

Diagram 9-26 shows an aggressive block by everyone except the left guard. The left guard is uncovered, therefore he shows pass for a one count and then blocks LB'er.

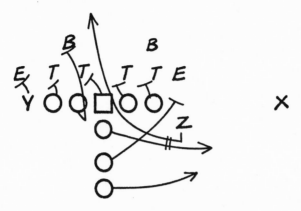

Diagram 9-26: Black-Left Draw to Z

Diagram 9-27 shows a fold technique against a 4-4 Defense by the right tackle. The center is the uncovered lineman, so he shows pass for a one count and blocks the offside LB'er. This play is very effective if the onside tackle can fold block tightly through center-guard gap in order to block the onside LB'er.

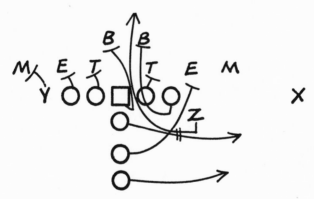

Diagram 9-27: Black-Left Draw to Z

10

Coordinating
the Passes and Screens

The passing series in the *Multiple-Motion I Offense* is comprised of three components: 60 Series (short passes), 70 Series (dropback), and the 80 Series (sprint-out). Chapter 6 described the pattern and the responsibilities of the receivers. Chapter 10 will focus on the strategical aspects of the 60, 70, and 80 Series in the *Multiple-Motion I Offense.*

60 SERIES

The 60 Series is the sequential plays to the 70 and 80 Series. The sequencing of 60 pass plays is comparable to sequencing running plays. In order for the defensive secondaries to respect your passing game, you must be able to pass short, medium, or long. Defensive backs have to be kept off-balance to insure unaggressive secondary play. Multiplicity in offensive attacks cannot be limited to just a varied running game. Multiplicity in offense is varied both in passing and running.

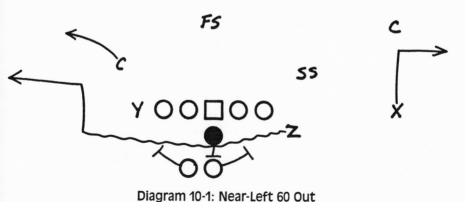

Diagram 10-1: Near-Left 60 Out

The 60 Series employs only three routes: slant, hitch, and out. These routes are run by X and Z only. Y always blocks on 60 patterns. In addition to the routes mentioned, motion by Z is automatic in all 60 series plays. Moreover, black formation is automatic. Diagrams 10-1, 10-2, and 10-3 illustrate the three 60 patterns.

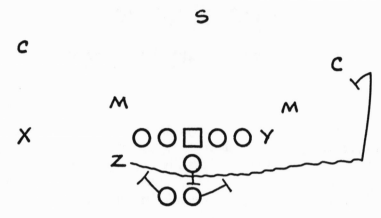

Diagram 10-2: Far-Right 60 Hitch

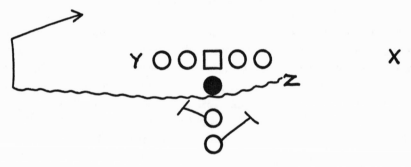

Diagram 10-3: Left 60 Slant

Blocking Rules

ON TACKLE:	2.
ON GUARD:	1.
CENTER:	0; off-side.
OFF GUARD:	1 over or outside; otherwise 2 ("If").
OFF TACKLE:	2 over or outside; otherwise 3 ("If").
Y:	3.
X:	Pattern called.
Z:	Pattern called.

NEAR BACK:	Widest man on L.O.S. aggressively.
FAR BACK:	Widest man on L.O.S. aggressively.
QUARTERBACK ACTION AND ALERTS:	3 step pocket action—throw to side with least pressure.

When should you use the 60 Series?

1. Defensive backs are playing deep.
2. Defensive backs are rotating to a 2-deep zone.
3. Outside LB'ers are playing close to L.O.S. thereby leaving passing lanes open.
4. Man-to-man coverage because defensive backs are so conscious of getting beat deep since they have no zone help.
5. Prevent defenses allow 60 out patterns (Beat the clock).
6. Goal-line territory requires a short passing game such as the 60 Series because of the limited space within the end zone and the man-to-man coverage that is normally employed with goal-line defense.

The 60 Series gives the quarterback an early read on a team's secondary coverage. With Z in motion, the quarterback can see secondary adjust. The split-end (X) is normally the receiver who will catch the ball because most secondaries will swing with Z as he goes in motion to Y's side. The quarterback always passes to the receiver who has no double coverage. Diagrams 10-4, 10-5, and 10-6 illustrate who the quarterback should pass to.

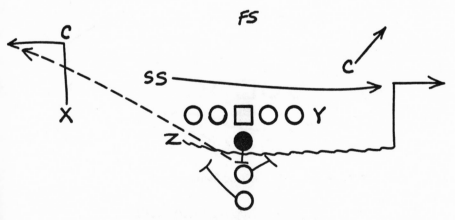

Diagram 10-4: Right 60 Out

Diagram 10-4 shows a conventional 4 deep secondary. As Z goes in motion, the strong safety follows. This key immediately tells the quarterback that the split-end (X) has single coverage and should be the primary receiver. If the strong safety doesn't follow in a "concerned" matter and is out of position for the flat, Z will be open for the out.

Diagram 10-5 illustrates a 3-deep secondary with the outside LB'ers dropping off into passing lanes if confronted with 2 receiver side. The Quarterback has no strong-safety to read. The quarterback's key is to pass to the side in which no LB'er has dropped off. As Z goes in motion, the quarterback can easily see if the LB'er on X's side remains off the L.O.S. If the LB'er remains in his original defensive position, the quarterback quickly keys the side that Z is going in motion to. If the LB'er stays on the L.O.S. and doesn't drop off when Z goes in motion to his side, the quarterback will immediately focus his passing to Z. However, if the LB'er does drop off, the quarterback will throw the ball away to the short side of the field. The defense is well prepared for the 60-slant. Therefore, the offense must learn to adjust and not attempt to pass through it. For passing through a coverage that is well suited to your pass, play will only result in offensive breakdowns. In Diagram 10-5, the 60 out to Z could be a possibility with the corners playing a 3-deep and the LB'ers off the L.O.S. but not in the flat territory. The *Multiple-Motion I Offense*, however, will not attempt this play because of the dangerous position of the outside LB'er. Passes are always available if the offense will adjust and not attempt to force the ball through coverages.

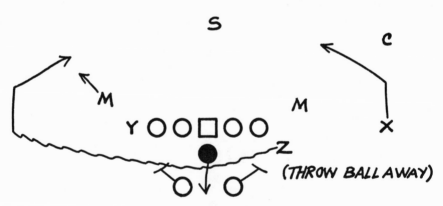

Diagram 10-5: Split-Left 60 Slant (throw ball away)

Diagram 10-6 shows a 4-deep secondary that is inverting. Regardless of the strong safety's movement to middle ⅓ responsibility, the quarterback upon reading the strong safety key (leaving area) will pass to X's side.

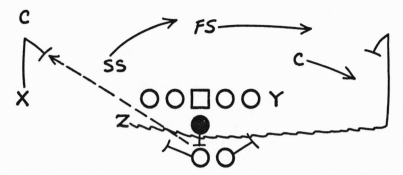

Diagram 10-6: Near-Right 60 Hitch

Many defensive teams that employ the popular 5-2 Defense will drop off their defensive end on the split-end side. This defensive maneuver allows the defense to play the passing zones on short passes. The *Multiple-Motion I Offense* attempts to confuse these defenses by surprising the defense with motion away from the split-end side. (See Diagram 10-7.) The black formation originally gives the defensive end a strong-side appearance towards the split-end side. Motion away from X ends ultimately in a standard pro-set look. If the defensive end reacts to the motion and drops off into flat territory, the quarterback will throw the ball away. (See Diagram 10-8.)

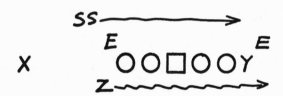

Diagram 10-7: (QB passes to X because def. end didn't drop off.)

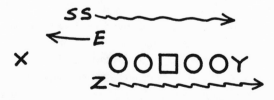

Diagram 10-8: (QB passes ball away)

70 SERIES

The 70 Series is the drop-back passing game of the *Multiple-Motion I Offense*. If an offense expects to stretch a defensive secondary so that it must cover sideline-to-sideline, a drop-back attack is necessary. The 70 Series as described in Chapter 6 consists of a multitude of passing combinations with a minimum of learning for the receivers and the quarterback. Because the 70 Series can literally dissect a defensive secondary with its multiplicity of plays, coaching strategy is vital.

The following diagrams will illustrate the use of the 70 Series and why certain plays were called. (See Diagram 10-9.)

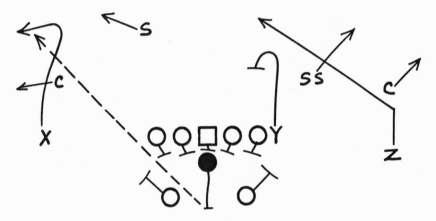

Diagram 10-9: Split-Right 73 Comeback

Diagram 10-9 illustrates the weakness of the 2-deep zone with cloud coverage. With both corners playing the short zone and the safeties playing a 2-deep zone, the comeback route to X is a great play to call. Z's post route also gives both safeties a genuine deep concern. This concern allows X to have great space to operate in. If the right defensive corner after attempting to delay X on his route begins to drift to his outside shoulder to squeeze the passing lane down on the comeback route to X, right 73 curl will be called. (See Diagram 10-10.)

Right 73 curl takes advantage of the corner's outside shuffle to stop the comeback route. The 70 Series can employ almost any pattern to overcome defensive weaknesses and still maintain offensive consistency. Offensive passing breakdowns occur because of the heavy mental load placed on receivers to understand and react to changing defensive secondaries. Although defensive secondaries can change their defenses on numerous occasions, the 70 Series with its multiplicity never places a heavy burden mentally on its offensive performers because they have only one thing to memorize (Chapter 6). The pressure of thinking and developing strategy is placed where it should be—the coaches' shoulders.

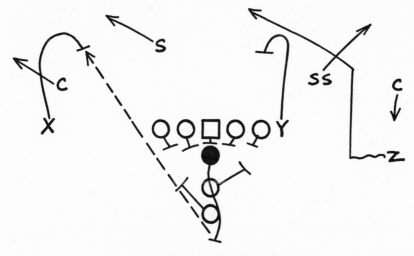

Diagram 10-10: Right 173 Curl

Diagram 10-11 shows a 70 pass play that exploits a weakness of the 3-deep zone coverage. Z in motion doesn't affect the 3-deep zone coverage as it does the 4-deep secondaries. Z, however, affects the secondary's concentration on who is moving (motion) and his route as he goes upfield

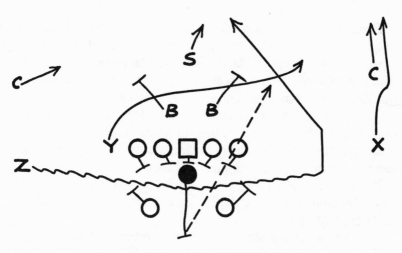

Diagram 10-11: Split-Left 272 Diagonal

in his post route. This deep post by Z and X's up pattern allows Y to run his diagonal pattern with great space between LB'er coverage and the secondary's 3-deep zone.

Diagram 10-12 uses the Black-Right 71 Diagonal as a passing play to show the versatility of the 70 Series. Diagram 10-12 is the same play as Diagram 10-11 except the flanker is now the primary receiver instead of the tight-end. In Diagram 10-12, the 71 Diagonal is being run against a standard 5-2 Monster defense. Y's hook pattern occupies the left-side LB'er enough that Z's diagonal will be wide open with the left corner playing his deep outside ⅓.

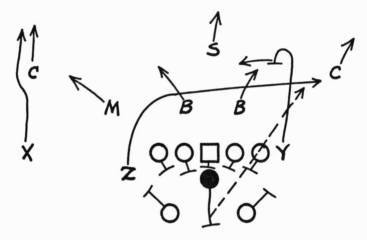

Diagram 10-12: Split-Black-Right 71 Diagonal

Diagram 10-13 shows a 70 Series pass play against man-to-man coverage. With Z in motion and also being the primary receiver in the Flat pattern, the success of Black Right 271 Flat is great because of the difficulty for the secondary to get proper defensive man-to-man alignment. Moreover, Z has a running start towards the flat area whereas the strong safety has to react to his motion first and then follow as quickly as possible to maintain proper man-to-man leverage. Y's hook pattern not only occupies the corner back, but the free safety must respect Y's inside release and pattern-direction towards his area.

If Y's hook route is occupying the free safety too much, a sequential 70 pass play from Black-Right 271 Flat can score an easy touchdown. (See Diagram 10-14.)

Any time a passing attack can isolate a receiver one-on-one with a defensive back and the defensive back has no help on the inside, the post

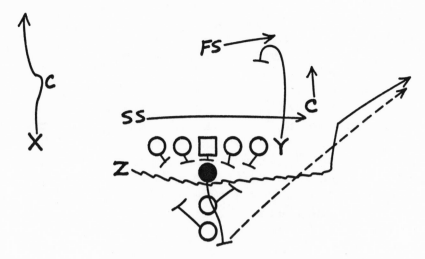

Diagram 10-13: Black-Right 271 Flat

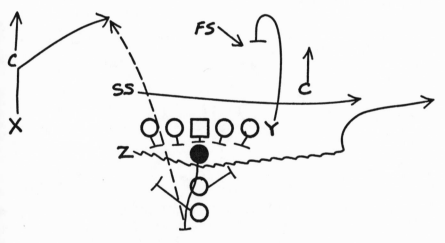

Diagram 10-14: Black-Right 273 Post

pattern is one of the most dangerous patterns an offense can run against any defense. Diagram 10-13 helps to set up the defense for play in Diagram 10-14. In Diagram 10-13, X's route was an up pattern which all defensive backs are always conscious of stopping. With X now running the post route and the corner expecting help from the free safety, the post route is excellent because the free safety has been creeping up on Y in his hook route.

The significance of the 70 Series is that the coaching staff can literally make up any combination of pass patterns utilizing X, Y, Z and create no extra hours of practice or chalk talks for the players. In addition to the myraid of plays available, motion can or can't be added on every play and the passing series remains constant. Within this Chapter hundreds of 70 Series pass plays could be drawn without any extra learning on anyone's part. The only requirement needed to operate the 70 Series effectively is to call pass plays that have a purpose.

Diagrams 10-15 to 10-17 illustrate more pass plays that can be utilized against conventional 3-deep and 4-deep zones.

When utilizing the twin set with the 70 Series, very often the word "flex" will be added. Flex tells Y to split out from 4-8 yds. depending on the hash mark. This flex allows Y to operate more freely from the L.O.S. and establish a pattern quicker. Diagram 10-18 is an example of how a big tight end could be isolated with a smaller defensive back one-on-one.

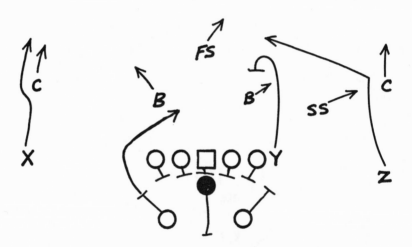

Diagram 10-15: Split-Right 70 Circle
(Isolate back on deep LB'er drop)

70 Blocking Rules

ONSIDE GUARD:	Inside gap; determines depth
ONSIDE TACKLE:	Inside gap; determines width
CENTER:	Block closest inside pressure
OFFSIDE GUARD:	Inside gap; determines depth
OFFSIDE TACKLE:	Inside gap; determines width
FB:	Block outside of tackle
TB:	Block outside of tackle (opposite of direction called)

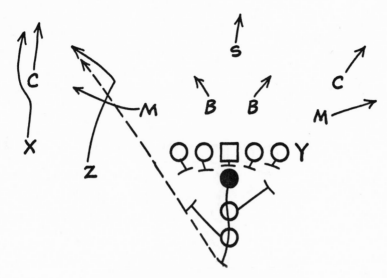

Diagram 10-16: Twins-Right 71 Flag
(Z is open in the dead area)

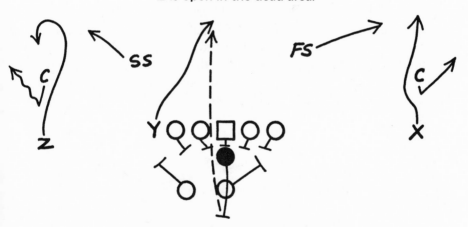

Diagram 10-17: Near-Left 72 Go
(Take advantage of Double Coverage)

80 SERIES

The 80 Series is the sprint-out passing game of the *Multiple-Motion I Offense*. Whereas, the 70 Series requires the secondary to play sideline to sideline, the 80 Series requires the defensive perimeter of team's defenses (defensive end, outside LB'er, C) to execute with tremendous responsibility and pressure. Moreover, the 80 Series is vital to the

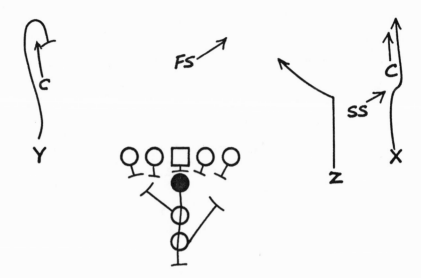

Diagram 10-18: Twins-Left Flex 72 Hook

sequencing of running plays in the *Multiple-Motion I Offense* (sprint-draw as an example). The Semi-sprint out though is the action of the quarterback not a complete sprint-out to the sideline. The semi-sprint utilized in the 80 Series is employed so that the quarterback can always pass to the secondary receiver on a crossing pattern. This maneuver is necessary so the free safety will not be able to slide to the outside so freely. (See Diagram 10-19.)

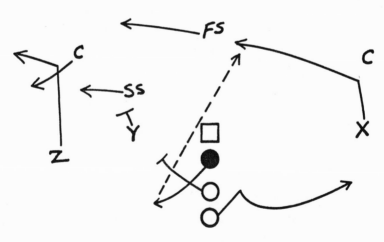

Diagram 10-19: Left 81 Square

In Diagram 10-19, the quarterback, upon seeing that Z is covered, will be able to hit X on his crossing pattern (Chapter 6) because the free safety has been cheating to strong-side flow to back up the corner on deep patterns. This cheating by the free safety explains why the corner is able to play the square pattern so well because he knows the free safety will help him deep. If the quarterback had a complete sprint-out, the crossing pattern by X would be almost impossible for the quarterback to see or

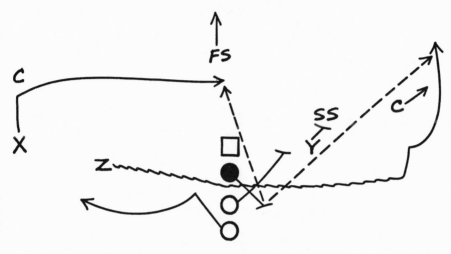

Diagram 10-20: Black-Right 282 Sideline

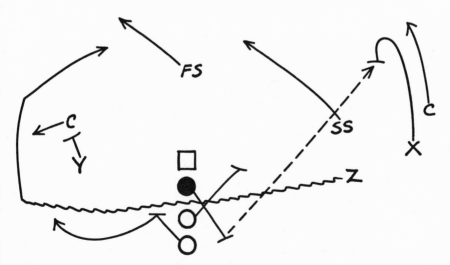

Diagram 10-21: Twins-Left 182 Hook

execute in time. The 81-82 gives the quarterback the opportunity to call any pattern individually with secondary receivers always crossing in the middle ⅓. See Diagrams 10-20 and 10-21 for further examples of the 81-82 series.

The 83-84 Floods are designed for two purposes: to flood a zone or isolate a skilled player one-on-one with a LB'er. Diagrams 10-22 and 10-23 illustrate the flooding of a zone.

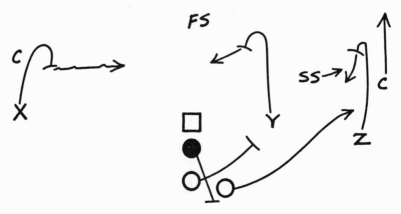

Diagram 10-22: Near-Right 84 Flood

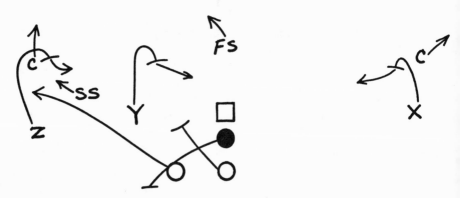

Diagram 10-23: Near-Left 83 Flood

Diagrams 10-22 and 10-23 are plays that put pressure on the defensive perimeter to stop. Can the corner stop the hook to Z? Can the inside LB'er read the seam to Y? Can the strong safety adjust to the back out of the backfield? Will the strong safety's adjustment to the back out of the backfield create a passing lane for Z on his hook? Can the free safety disregard X on his hook pattern? If motion, will it be real or a decoy?

Diagrams 10-24 and 10-25 demonstrate the other purpose of the flood pattern—to attack weakside and create pressure on the inside LB'er.

Diagram 10-24 illustrates a 5-2 Monster secondary set up. This alignment forces the inside LB'er away from 2 receiver side to play the near back man-to-man, since X is streaking and clearing out with defensive corner-back following. If an offensive team can isolate this offensive maneuver in a game a few times, the offense should be able to generate some points.

Diagram 10-25 is an example of how the quarterback must react to secondary play. When Z was in motion, the corner remained tight to X's

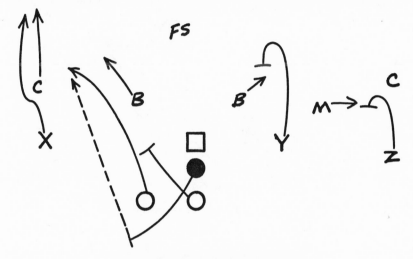

Diagram 10-24: Far-Right 83 Flood

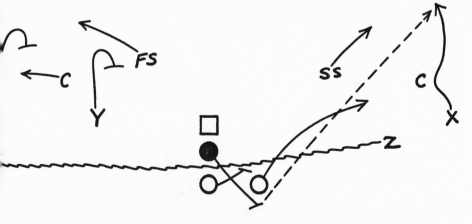

Diagram 10-25: Twins-Far-Left 184 Flood

side which indicated a 2 deep coverage. Since the corner back had the flat area covered, X must run his go pattern quickly and correctly to beat the safety on the go pattern. Furthermore, since there is no inside help, Z should be able to run a very good hook and slide pattern.

A sequential passing series to the 83-84 Flood plays is the 83-84. As Chapter 6 described, the 83-84 Series is designed to read the strong safety coverage and inside LB'er coverage. The 83-84 Series is excellent versus defenses that utilize LB'ers in short, straight-back drops. This maneuver allows Y to be free very often. (See Diagram 10-26)

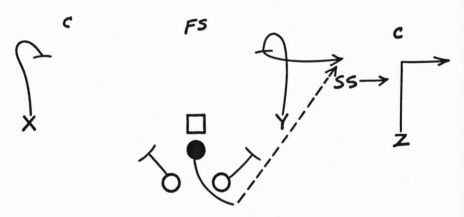

Diagram 10-26: Split-Right 84

80 Blocking Rules

ON TACKLE:	2.
ON GUARD:	1.
CENTER:	0; off-side.
OFF GUARD:	1 over or outside; otherwise 2 ("If").
OFF TACKLE:	2 over or outside; otherwise 3 ("If").
Y:	Pattern or block.
X:	Pattern.
Z:	Pattern.
NEAR BACK:	Block to side of play.
FAR BACK:	Block backside; flare if LB'er doesn't come; if flood is called, always block onside.

SCREEN TO TAILBACK AND FULLBACK

The screen series in any offense can only be successful if the defense is vulnerable to it. To call a screen because it seems like a good time (second and 15 yds. to go) takes away from any strategical sequencing that you as a coach must employ to be sound offensively. The screen will take advantage of a blitzing type defense as well as a read-type defense if properly executed. However, the key to screen success in any offense is to predict what the defense will do and execute. Diagram 10-27 demonstrates a screen against a 5-2 Monster defense, whereby the monster is playing toward the 2 receiver's side.

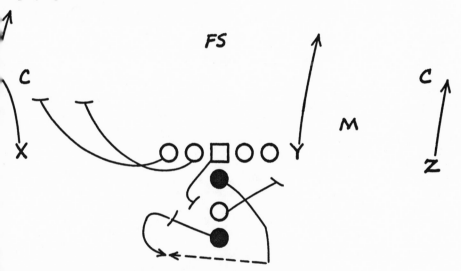

Diagram 10-27: Right-Screen Left

Diagram 10-28 illustrates the screen to the fullback because the monster is now playing the wide side of the field and not the 2 receiver side.

If the defensive end on the split end side is playing a walk-away position from his counter-part, the monster (2-receiver side), the *Multiple-Motion I Offense* utilizes a running screen to the fullback. (See Diagram 10-29.)

This underneath screen by the fullback takes advantage of the defensive end who is keying on the tailback in his flat area. The word running is applied because the fullback will catch the ball running parallel to the L.O.S. and usually near the center area. The screen tackle

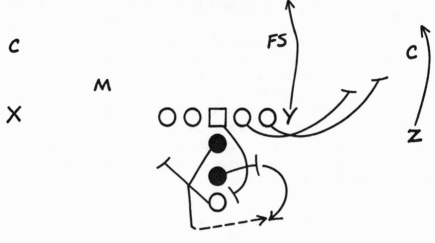

Diagram 10-28: Right-Screen Right

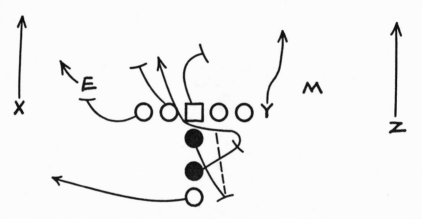

Diagram 10-29: Right-Fullback Screen Left

will simply seal off the defensive end in his flat coverage, and the screen guard and center will lead through for the fullback.

TIGHT-END SCREEN

The screen to Y (tight-end) is a great play if some key concepts are employed and understood:

1. Screen has to be to narrow side. The reason being that secondary coverage is off the L.O.S. more and the defensive end play is more aggressive to narrow side.

2. Y must be employed as a blocker on pass patterns such as the 81-82 Series so that the defense will be accustomed to seeing Y stay in to block.

3. Secondary play must be aware of a passing attack that has been placing pressure on all 3-deep zone areas. If the offense has been passing the ball short and infrequent, the Y screen will be a disaster.

4. X and Z must be in a twins set away from Y so that no strong safety or monster will be in flat area for their 2 man pass responsibility. Y must have single coverage to insure against quick reads from short zone areas. (See Diagrams 10-30 and 10-31.)

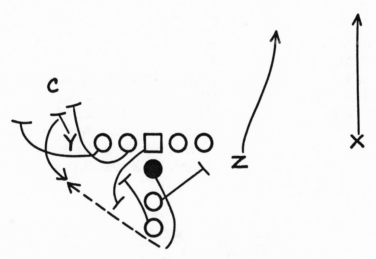

Diagram 10-30: Black-Left Screen Left to P

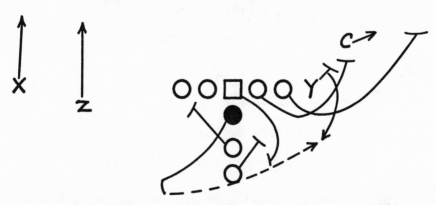

Diagram 10-31: Twins-Right Screen Right to P

FLANKER SCREEN

The screen to Z takes advantage of quick reads by defensive perimeter people on the outside screens to the tailback and fullback. See Diagram 10-32 for the development of screen to Z.

This screen to Z over the middle is very successful on defensive teams that read well. The screen area exploited by the *Multiple-Motion I Offense* is the defensive area where the fake key has been flashed. When the tailback flares to the flat, the defensive end and LB'er to that area fly to the outside thereby creating more room for Z over the middle. The key block is the center who must read the backside LB'er and seal him off from Z when Z is receiving the ball.

Screen Blocking Rules

ON TACKLE: 2.
ON GUARD: 1.
CENTER: 0; off-side-2 count; peel man in screen.
OFF GUARD: ("If")-2 count; form screen
OFF TACKLE: ("If")-2 count; form screen
Y: Release, block most dangerous man.
X: Release, block most dangerous man.
Z: Release, block most dangerous man.

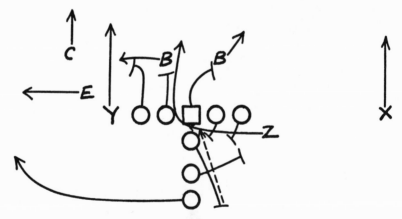

Diagram 10-32: Black-Left Screen to Z

ATTACKING 2-DEEP WITH Y MOTION

The 2-deep secondary has become increasingly popular with college and high school coaches since the NFL has had so much success using it.

Before, many coaches thought that the 2-deep secondary was too vulnerable for good passing teams. To clarify the 2-deep secondary, the cornerbacks are rolled up tight on the wide receivers, attempting to bump and funnel the receivers into the two safeties' area who are playing the two deep halves of the field. Diagram 10-33 demonstrates the 2-deep.

It is not the book's intention to describe the many variations of the 2-deep secondary play. The purpose of the *Multiple-Motion I Offense* is to show how to attack defenses and make them predictable. The 2-deep can be played with several adjustments. The offensive purpose is not to probe until the offense thinks it knows the total 2-deep play of a defense, but to do things offensively that will force the defense to change its defense to be simplistic.

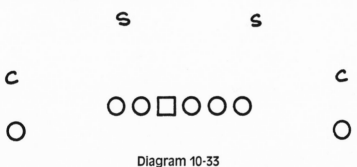

Diagram 10-33

The key in the *Multiple-Motion I Offense* is to use the tight-end (Y) to break up 2-deep secondaries. As detailed in Chapter 1, (Y) goes in motion on 700 or 800 digits. The Multiple-Motion I Offense puts (Y) in motion so that he cannot be held up at the LOS and can also cause concern for the defense—he can be used as an extra blocker to create an unbalanced formation if he goes in motion toward 2 receivers. Diagram 10-34 demonstrates.

With (Y) in motion, it enables a receiver to break more clearly from the LOS and get into deep zones earlier. Most defenses that play 2-deep are acutely aware that (Y) running a deep pattern will cause secondary problems. Therefore, the defense adjusts by delaying (Y)'s release from the LOS, thinking that by the time (Y) get loose, the pass rush will force the quarterback to run or pass off quickly.

Diagram 10-34 demonstrates the weakness of 2-deep coverage versus (Y) in motion. (X) stretches the cornerback and forces the safety to come over. (Y) reads the safety; if the safety is closing fast on (X), (Y) breaks at a 45° angle and looks for the ball. If the safety is trying to play both deep receivers, (Y) runs a legal "pick" and gets between the safety and (X), his teammate. The quarterback simply reads the safety to (Y)'s motion side. If the safety is closing quickly to (X)'s side, he looks to pass to (Y) on his 45° angle break. The safety, however, plays soft or hesitant; the quarterback passes to (X) using (Y) as a screen between (X) and the safety.

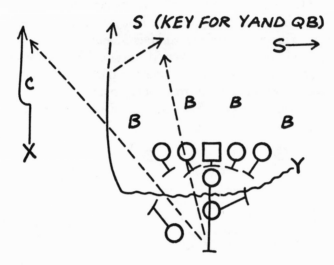

Diagram 10-34: Far-Right 772 Go

11

Drills for a Winning Program

The key concept in drills for a winning football program is that the drills must have a kinesthetic transfer from drill to game conditions. Moreover, the drills must be administered with teaching, not scolding, in mind.

The *Multiple-Motion I Offense's* drills are not unique or flamboyant. Its drills are employed with one purpose in mind: to make a football player become a better game player. Practice players and game players are two different kind of athletes. Game players are athletes who can transfer skills to competitive situations and excell.

Drills for a winning program cannot be picked at random so that a practice plan can be completed and the coaching staff look organized. Drills should have a direct input and feedback to the progress of a football team's philosophy and goals. Moreover, drills should be universal throughout a program—freshman through senior year. If a freshman completes his freshman football year, the following year as a sophomore, the drills should be more clearer to the athlete and most importantly of all—the purpose for doing the drills.

The following drills are broken down into four categories: offensive line, receivers, offensive backs, and quarterbacks.

OFFENSIVE LINE DRILLS

Shot Block Drill

EQUIPMENT: None
PURPOSE: To teach straight line explosion off the L.O.S. from a good stance.
PROCEDURE: The blocker assumes his fundamental offensive stance. On a snap count given

by the coach, he explodes out and in a straight line to and through the upper numbers of the defensive player. He does not move his feet. Defensive man is on one knee with the foot of that leg moved back in under his tail: upon contact, this man will collapse and be bowled over with no danger of injury. He should have his head turned to one side to eliminate any blow to his chin if the blocker is a little high in his contact.

EMPHASIZE: Stance.
                                        Quickness in reaction to snap count.
                                        Explosion from stance.

Perfect Block Drill

EQUIPMENT: No extra equipment needed.
PURPOSE: Leg drive, maintain balance, keep back straight, quick choppy steps.
PROCEDURE: Pair up players, blocker gets into a good stance with face into defensive man's mid section. The blocker will pick up hands up, defensive man holds blocker in position. On the signal the blocker churns feet and drives defensive man off boards. Defensive players offer full resistance.
EMPHASIZE: Driving feet, maintain balance, short choppy, do not over extend, do not get too high.

One-on-One Drill

EQUIPMENT: Two long dummies.
PURPOSE: Good explosion, leg drive, maintaining balance, *TOUGHNESS*.
PROCEDURE: Make a lane by laying two dummies parallel about two yards apart. The blocker should be about a yard from the defen-

sive man. Both should be a good stance. Blocker will go whenever he is ready. The blocker will drive the defender out of the area.

EMPHASIZE: Good explosion, contact point, leg drive, *TOUGHNESS*.

Approach Drill

EQUIPMENT: Light weight bell dummies, boards, bolders, and blockers.

PURPOSE:
1. Explosion off L.O.S.
2. Run 100 yard dash through the contact point and beyond with the head and back at the same level throughout.
3. Ignite (accelerate) at contact point.

PROCEDURE: Blocker is in a good hitting stance (four point) about 1 to 2 yards from the dummy. On the snap count, the blocker explodes off the L.O.S. with his head aimed at the middle of the dummy at crotch height. Explode into and through the dummy for 3 to 5 steps. Stop under control remaining on the dummy. You may freeze him so as to keep it consistent.

CHECK: Blocker should be in the same relative position as in the original stance except the hands should be off the ground.

Thud Drill

EQUIPMENT: Boards, defenders, blockers.

PURPOSE:
1. To execute sprint blocking techniques "live."
2. To teach the blocker to *explode* through the defender's "unload."
3. To teach the blocker to sustain his block for *at least 5 yards*.

PROCEDURE: The blocker assumes his stance, strad-
                    dling the board opposite the defender in
                    a 3 or 4 point stance. On the snap count
                    the blocker explodes through the *face*
                    mask and into the crotch of the defender.
                    The defender should unload on the
                    blocker, but then become passive follow-
                    ing his "unload" which will allow the
                    blocker to drive him. Drive the defender
                    off the board and downfield for *at least 5*
                    yards.
EMPHASIZE: *EXPLOSION, ACCELERATION,*
                    BUST FANNY, WORK YOUR
                    HEAD UP.

Reflex Drill

EQUIPMENT: Boards, defenders, blockers.
PURPOSE: To teach a blocker to react to a defender
                    releasing off block for pursuit angle.
PROCEDURE: 1. Coach indicates direction of pursuit to
                       defense.
                    2. Defender should "thud" blocker then
                       become passive. When coach yells
                       "REFLEX," defender must give
                       ground in the direction previously
                       indicated.
                    3. Blocker must explode defender off
                       the board. The blocker should imme-
                       diately react to the defender's angle
                       change by driving the head across the
                       far knee and accelerating ("put it in
                       high gear") to sustain a position be-
                       tween the defender and the ball car-
                       rier. *STAY IN FOUR RUNNING*
                       GEARS.
EMPHASIZE: Staying in the defender's running gears
                    and 2nd, 3rd and 4th effort.

Stunt Drill

EQUIPMENT: No special equipment required.

PURPOSE: To acquaint players with blocking, stacks and stunts.

PROCEDURE: Align players into desired working area such as center and guards vs. middle LB'er and two technique. (See Diagram 11-1.) Coach stands behind offense and indicates type of stunt desired. On snap of ball the defense executes the stunt. Offensive personnel must block the man who stunts into his area.

EMPHASIZE: Keeping eyes open and blocking an area. Get off ball and be ready for stunt.

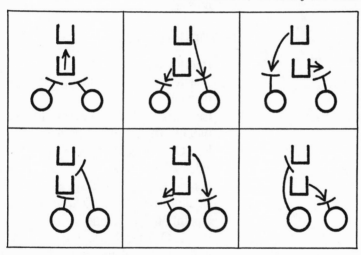

Diagram 11-1: Stunt Drill

Effort Drill

EQUIPMENT: 7 boards, offensive line, 7 defenders, 3 to 4 bell dummies.

PURPOSE: To check alignment, stance, explosion, blocking through defender, 6 second maximum effort.

PROCEDURE: Align 7 boards vertical to the L.O.S. and a defender in a down position on each board. On snap, offense explodes into defense and drives him off the board; offside linemen drive their men off, then run through bell dummies. This is good for conditioning and effort emphasis.

CHECK: Stance, alignment, explosion, effort, feet action, desire to block opponent, staying low.

COACHING POINTS: Usually best and more worthwhile at end of practice. Have lots of enthusiasm, set up contests, no loafers, great for morale.

Interception Drill

EQUIPMENT: Interior line, footballs.

PURPOSE: Teach proper coverage after a pass is thrown.

PROCEDURE: Call play, allow linemen to execute blocks, then yell cover right or cover left. Onside tackle goes to a point on the sideline which will make him 5 yards behind L.O.S.; onside guard goes to the sideline down the L.O.S.; center goes to a point on the sideline 5 yards in front of the L.O.S.; off-side guard goes to a point on the sideline 10 yards in front of the L.O.S.; and the offside tackle goes to a point on the sideline 15 yards in front of L.O.S.

EMPHASIZE: Importance of coverage, quickness in locating ball, readiness to tackle.

RECEIVER DRILLS

Eye-on-Ball Drill

EQUIPMENT: Footballs, groups of 4 receivers.

PURPOSE: To teach and improve concentration on

	the catching of the football. Catch it in fingers and tuck away.
PROCEDURE:	Place 2 receivers facing each other approximately 15 yards apart. Immediately in front of each place a defender, upright facing one another. One receiver passes the ball to the other. The defender in front of the receiver yells, makes arm and hand motions at ball without touching it. This forces the receiver to concentrate on the ball rather than other distracting things. He should catch ball in his hands and tuck away and then throw it back to the other receiver who will be harrassed by the defender in front of him. You may send them across the field and back. Then switch and repeat.
CHECK:	Catching in hands, eyes; tucking it away.

Relaxation Drill

EQUIPMENT:	Receivers, footballs.
PURPOSE:	To teach and improve the "touch" of catching a football, tucking it away and sprinting 5 more yards. Catch it with the fingers—gently.
PROCEDURE:	Set up drill as diagrammed in 11-2. Coach passes ball crisply, not hard or soft. Throw the light type. Receivers should catch ball with fingers of the one hand until they go deep, then use fingers of both hands with elbows close together. They then move across from right to left and then left to right.
CHECK:	Finger control. agility of turning when throwing behind the receiver. 5 yards after catching.
COACHING POINTS:	Count number of receptions in a row.

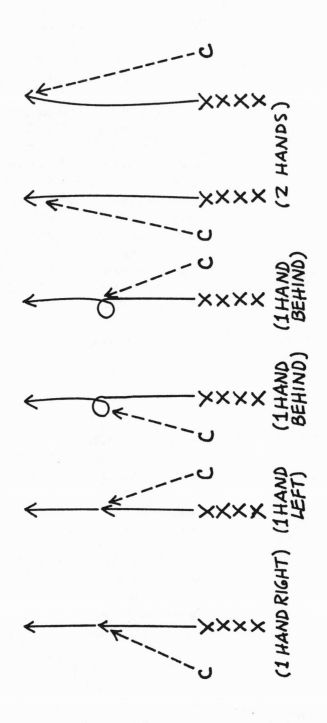

Diagram 11-2: Relaxation Drill

Concentration Drill

EQUIPMENT: Footballs, receivers.

PURPOSE: To develop concentration and confidence in catching the ball with distractions around.

PROCEDURE: Set up 2 lines of receivers parallel to each other. Each line should be 5 yards apart. Separate both lines and have the lead people run towards each side's field. Passer will pass when both people are even. The front person waves but *doesn't* touch the ball.

CHECK: Eye concentration and running with purpose in mind.

COACHING POINTS: Don't run with arms outstretched till last possible moment. Look ball in before running.

Smash Drill

EQUIPMENT: 2 air dummies, 2 holders, footballs, receivers.

PURPOSE: To develop concentration on catching the football. Moreover, improve toughness in getting to the ball.

PROCEDURE: Set up a line of receivers facing the passer and 2 dummy holders. When passer yells "Go," the first receiver runs full speed through the dummy holders. Ball should be thrown when receiver is getting hit by the dummies.

CHECK: Continual foot movement, balance, aggressiveness, toughness.

COACHING POINTS: Keep body low. Keep elbows in. Catch ball first, then run.

Harass Drill

EQUIPMENT: Receivers, air dummies (optional), passer, footballs.

PURPOSE: To help receiver learn to concentrate on watching the ball with a defender bearing down on him.

PROCEDURE: Receiver moving at a controlled speed with defender coming straight at him. Ball is thrown in front of receiver so he has to reach for the ball. Defender comes straight on him and butts him tough.

COACHING POINTS: 1. Keep eyes on the ball.
                     2. Put it away.
                     3. Deliver a tough drop-shoulder on the defender and roll or spin on down field.

Turn Drill

EQUIPMENT: Footballs, receivers.

PURPOSE: To develop concentration and rotation of head and trunk when back is to the ball.

PROCEDURE: Set up a line of receivers facing passer 10 yards out. First receiver has back to passer. When passer yells "Turn," the ball will already be in the air. Second man then becomes the receiver and the last receiver goes to the end of the line.

CHECK: Hands are in proper position. Catch ball with hands then body.

COACHING POINTS: Good trunk rotation of lower torso. Hands are high when rotating around to catch, not held low near the waist.

Sideline Drill

EQUIPMENT: Footballs, receivers, and a chalk line indicating sideline markers.

PURPOSE:	To develop concentration in catching ball and staying in-bounds at the same time.
PROCEDURE:	Line of receivers facing a sideline from 7-8 yards away. Passer yells go and receiver races to sideline. Passer passes ball right near sideline.
CHECK:	Receivers are not slowing up. Natural stride till sideline get near.
COACHING POINTS:	Keep eyes on ball and tuck it away. Short choppy steps after receiving ball.

Somersault Drill

EQUIPMENT:	Receivers, footballs.
PURPOSE:	Increase quickness in getting off the ground.
PROCEDURE:	Start from your stance; take two or three quick steps forward, then somersault and up in a receiver's position. Coach or quarterback will throw to you just as you get up. This should all be done in a 5 yard area.
COACHING POINTS:	1. Throw ball firmly to receiver at different positions; let him get completely in position and also catch him off balance.
	2. Recover as quickly as possible.
	3. Whip head and look for ball.
	4. Tuck ball away and sprint 5 yards.

7-Up Drill

EQUIPMENT:	Footballs, receivers, quarterback, tacklers.
PURPOSE:	Develop concentration for the quarterback, proper technique of pass receiving, proper technique of ball carrying, conditioning and fumble recovery drill.

open field tackling, and pursuit-angle and sideline tackling.

PROCEDURE: The drill begins with toe quarterback standing on the goal line. Two lines of tacklers are 5 yards apart from the quarterback. Receivers and/or ball-carriers are lined up on the 25 yd. line in one single line facing the quarterback and tacklers. Quarterback initiates the drill by shouting "Go," and passing the ball with good snap-wrist action towards the first receiver who has started to run forward on the quarterback's "Go." The tacklers, like the receivers, also run forward as fast as they can on the word "Go."

EMPHASIZE: Catching the ball before running with it.

RUNNING BACK DRILLS

Maneuver Drill

EQUIPMENT: Bell dummy, mgr. to hold it, towel, footballs.

PURPOSE: To teach and improve a ball carrier's escape techniques, balance, development and use of the stiff arm, use of eyes, improvement in coordination and conditioning and the overall improvement of runners and their balance.

PROCEDURE: Set drill up as diagrammed in 11-3 with dummy 10 yards from the line of runners. Make certain that you mirror the drill if you can do so. Coach stands behind dummy with a towel to "pop" the runner's legs, Runners should sprint 5 yards past the coach.

CHECK: Run straight at dummy, knees high, use of stiff arm (don't cock pistol), overall balance, quickness, sprint after escape.

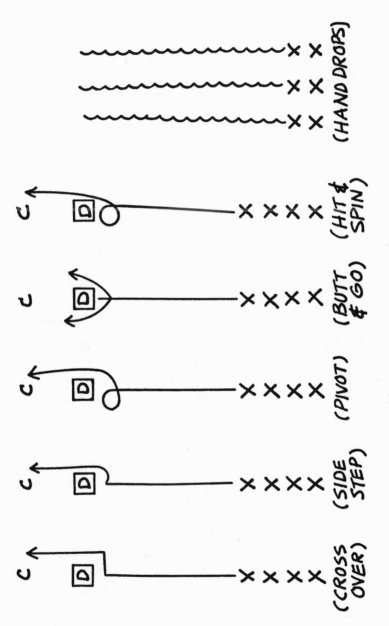

Diagram 11-3: Maneuver Drill

COACHING POINTS: The most important thing to emphasize is for the runner to keep his feet moving.

Blast Drill

EQUIPMENT: 2 large dummies, 2 dummy holders, footballs, quarterback, ball carriers.

PURPOSE: Hit handoff spot, quick, low, head up, and determined to score. Get in the end zone some way.

PROCEDURE: Let each ball carrier have one and only one blast at goal line. Dummy holders do everything in their power, with the dummy that each has, to keep ball carrier from scoring.

CHECK: Don't look for the ball; keep inside elbow up, keep knees high and feet moving continually, protect the football. Score at all costs.

COACHING POINTS: Make it a contest, have fun.

Fumble Drill

EQUIPMENT: Ball carriers, footballs, defenders, quarterbacks.

PURPOSE: To teach concentration, improve hand-offs, eliminate fumbles, to keep ball covered at all times.

PROCEDURE: Tackler should be on knee, with leg folded under, immediately in front of handoff spot. At handoff, tackler should make moderate contact with ball carrier, but square. Ball carrier goes through and down.

CHECK: His eyes, position of hands and arms at handoff, see that he does not put hand down to break fall.

COACHING POINTS: Ball carrier should be normal (not too low).

Score Drill

EQUIPMENT: 4 or 5 air dummies, 3 bell dummies, 6 to
                    8 snatchers, running backs, footballs.

PURPOSE: To develop and improve the ability to
                    keep feet moving, protect football, main-
                    tain balance, not look for ball at handoff.

PROCEDURE: Set drill up as diagrammed in 11-4 about
                    20 yards from the goal line. Quarterback
                    hands ball to ball carrier who blasts
                    through 2 bell dummies and runs be-
                    tween 2 lines of "grabbers" facing each
                    other. The grabbers snatch at the ball.

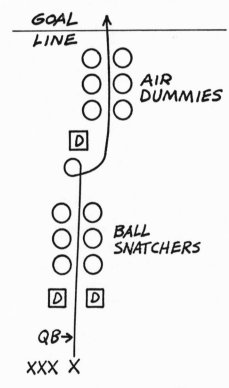

Diagram 11-4: Score Drill

After clearing them, runner sprints to bell dummy that is held by another who gives direction by tilting the bell dummy as to which side to break off of. Then runner sprints for "pay dirt," while remaining players throw air dummies at his knees and feet.

CHECK: Eyes and arm position at handoff, strength and body position blasting through bell dummies, maintaining balance and covering the ball while going through the grabbers, the move made against the bell dummy and knee action going in.

COACHING POINTS: Lots of enthusiasm.

Sideline Drill

EQUIPMENT: Backs, footballs, 3 to 4 dummies, 3 air dummies, and a cone.

PURPOSE: To teach backs to stay in-bounds and run tough down the sideline.

PROCEDURE: Organize the group with a line of ball carriers, and a line of dummy holders down the sideline. Ball carrier takes the ball and runs over the dummies about 5 yards apart and about 5 yards from sideline, then attempts to knock the ball carrier out-of-bounds. Ball carrier must be tough and try to stay in-bounds.

EMPHASIZE: Being tough, meeting tacklers, and staying inside as long as possible and then getting out-of-bounds.

Snatch Drill

EQUIPMENT: All running backs, quarterback, footballs, towel.

PURPOSE: To take ball properly, tuck it away and

keep it in proper position while running and being harassed by defenders.

PROCEDURE: Ball carrier advances and takes handoff sprinting between 2 lines with the defenders snatching at the ball with one hand. May put every other one on his knees, grabbing at ball carrier's knees with one hand.

CHECK: Eyes at handoff, pocket, proper coverage of the ball and it's placement. Balance, power and speed.

COACHING POINTS: Use towel to flip at runner's legs to make him make a break and sprint 5 more yards.

Burma Road Drill

EQUIPMENT: 4 air dummies, 4 holders, footballs, running backs.

PURPOSE: To develop and improve stamina, toughness, competitiveness, along with the use of various escapes. This is an excellent conditioner.

PROCEDURE: Set up 4 men with air or bell dummies, about 6 to 8 yards apart as diagrammed in 11-5. Give runner the ball and he flies to the first one and butts it in good tough running position; the dummy holder jolts him and tries to knock him down. He then proceeds to the next one and so on. After 4 backs have run, then switch the holders. This is jolting to them as well as the runner.

CHECK: Continual foot movement, balance, aggressiveness, toughness, condition, running low and with authority.

COACHING POINTS: Run full speed and butt them. Bounce back and go get the next one. Holders

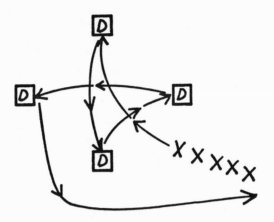

Diagram 11-5

should be real tough, so try to give them a jolt and cause them to lose their balance. This drill needs a lot of enthusiasm. Should be run near the end of practice when all backs are tired.

QUARTERBACK DRILLS

Globetrotter Drills

EQUIPMENT: Footballs, quarterbacks.

PURPOSE: To develop eye-to-hand coordination, stronger wrists and hands, and a "feeling" for the football.

PROCEDURE: Each quarterback begins by dropping and catching the football before it hits the ground with each hand 10 times. After this drill, the quarterback does a basketball figure-8 drill with the ball through his legs. After the firgure-8 drill, the ball is dropped between the legs and the quarterback attempts to catch the ball with arms behind his legs.

CHECK: Quarterbacks are going too slow in order to handle ball.

COACHING POINTS: Quickness with legs and hands to develop the coordination necessary to be a good quarterback.

One-Knee Passing Drill

EQUIPMENT: Footballs, quarterbacks.

PURPOSE: To develop correct throwing procedure.

PROCEDURE: Two quarterbacks, 10 yards apart, each with one knee down, passing a football to each other.

CHECK: Are quarterbacks attempting to hit spots?

COACHING POINTS: If throwing arm goes across the chest, incorrect passing form. Arm should follow through to the ground.

Number Passing Drill

EQUIPMENT: Footballs, receivers, quarterbacks.

PURPOSE: To develop an awareness for open man.

PROCEDURE: A line of 5-6 receivers facing a quarterback 15-18 yards apart.Quarterback releases ball to the receiver who raises both hands. All receivers will be raising an arm or jumping, but only one will raise both arms.

CHECK: Receivers are performing their technique and not cheating on receiving the ball.

COACHING POINTS: Quarterback is not dropping arm in deciding who to pass to. Moreover, the steps involved should not be very many. Only 1 to 2 steps allowed. Quarterbacks must keep weight back.

Pitch Drill

EQUIPMENT: Quarterbacks, footballs.

PURPOSE: To develop an option pitch that is accurate and quick.

PROCEDURE: Pair quarterbacks so that they are 5
                          yards apart and facing the same direc-
                          tion. Quarterbacks then run toward the
                          sideline, pitching the ball to each other.
                          At the end of sideline, reverse direction
                          and continue so that each quarterback
                          will practice both hands in pitching.

CHECK: Are the pitches high or low? Is quarter-
                          back running full speed?

COACHING POINTS: Quarterback must break down and
                          pitch. Hand and arm must extend and
                          follow through to target.

Index